Natural Gourmet

If you live within driving distance of The Natural Gourmet, here's how to get there from nearby Massachusetts, Connecticut and New York:

Take the Mass. Turnpike to Interstate 495, north to Route 2; east on 2 to Concord, then west on Route 62 to West Concord. Bear right at the 99 Restaurant and look for The Natural Gourmet on the right. From the Boston area, take Route 2 west to Route 62 at Concord, and then as above.

Too far away? Try this sample of The Natural Gourmet's fare in your own kitchen—or indulge yourself and get it from The Natural Gourmet at 1-800-542-2898 or 508 371-7573.

DEB'S GRANOLA

Makes 12 servings

1/2 cup unsweetend coconut	1/4 cups wheat bran
3 cups sliced almonds	☐
2 cups rolled oats	1 cup maple syrup
1 cup wheat flakes	1/4 cup canola or safflower oil
1 cup rye flakes	1 teaspoon vanilla extract
1 cup barley flakes	1/4 teaspoon salt, optional

Preheat oven to 300 degrees.

Mix dry ingredients in a large bowl. (If you don't have a large enough bowl, divide dry ingredients between two, for example, 1 cup rolled oats in one bowl, and 1 cup oats in a second.) Pour wet ingredients over dry and mix well using your hands or a rubber spatula. Make sure all the grains are well-coated.

Spread granola in shallow pans and bake in the oven until golden brown and dry, about 1-1/2 hours. Stir every 15-20 minutes. Baking time varies due to weather, the size of your pans, your oven, etc.

When granola is dry and golden brown, remove from oven and stir. Let cool completely before storing in airtight containers.

ROUND-THE-WORLD COOKING
AT
THE NATURAL GOURMET

Cookbooks from Keats

Candida Albicans · Pat Connolly and Associates of the
Yeast-Free Cookbook   Price-Pottenger Foundation

Cooking With Mrs. · Louise Andrews Kent and
Appleyard   Elizabeth Kent Gay

Cooking with Vitamins · Martha Oliver

The Family Whole Grain · Beatrice Trum Hunter
Baking Book

Loaves and Fishes · Janet Crisler and Malvina Kinard

Meals and Menus for All · Agnes Toms
Seasons

Natural Foods Blender · Frieda Nusz
Cookbook

Round-The-World Cooking at The Natural Gourmet

DEBRA STARK

Keats Publishing, Inc. New Canaan, Connecticut

ROUND-THE-WORLD COOKING AT THE NATURAL GOURMET

Copyright © 1991, 1994 by The Natural Gourmet. Originally published in slightly different form by Scarecrow Enterprises in 1991 as *Cooking at The Natural Gourmet.* Published by arrangement with the author.

Library of Congress Cataloging-in-Publication Data

Stark, Debra.
    Round-the-world cooking at the Natural Gourmet / Debra Stark.
        p.   cm.
    "Originally published in slightly different form by Scarecrow
Enterprises in 1991 as Cooking at the Natural Gourmet"—Galley verso t.p.
    Includes index.
    1. Cookery (Natural foods)   2. Cookery, International.   3. Natural
Gourmet (Store)   I. Natural Gourmet (Store)   II. Title.
III. Title: Cooking at the Natural Gourmet.
    TX741.S73   1994
    641.5'63—dc20   93-48569
                                                                        CIP

Printed in the United States of America

Published by Keats Publishing, Inc.
27 Pine Street (Box 876)
New Canaan, Connecticut 06840-0876

Acknowledgments

My love to my parents, Beatrice and Sidney Stark, and to my brothers, David and Daniel Stark, without whom there would be no Natural Gourmet. And to my son, Adam, who has helped eat the bloopers during the two years it took to compile this book.

Special thanks to Mary Kadlik and Amy Jenner for their aid in testing recipes and offering valuable criticisms. We struggled through Nutritionist III together.

And for their encouragement, patience and help in editing while the book was being put together, the staff at The Natural Gourmet deserve a big hug: Dale Berlied, Nancy Noorigian, Adelpha Abrahamson, Jan Milgroom, Johanna Beicke and Susan Kafalas.

My gratitude to Neal Higgins of Neal Higgins Studio, Atlanta, Georgia for the lovely cover photograph, and to my brother, David, who played creative consultant.

And last, but not least, thanks to our fans in the store, who not only asked that we write a cookbook, but who tasted, gave us honest feedback and kept coming to support us. Your warmth and friendship kept us going. We have the largest extended family of anyone I know.

Contents

Preface

The Natural Gourmet, located in West Concord, Massachusetts, opened in October, 1989. Most of the recipes in this book are prepared and served in our kitchen for take-out. We have also included dishes which we love but cannot make in the store, because they need to be prepared and served immediately.

Together, we have been exploring natural foods, becoming aware that in our modern, technological society, we have been eating too much, enjoying food too little, and getting a poor return for our dollars spent and calories consumed. This book celebrates natural foods from around the world. May you have fun preparing these recipes and sharing them with family and friends.

All recipes are scaled down to home use.

Yours in health and happiness!

Round-The-World Cooking at THE NATURAL GOURMET

Introduction

I was fortunate to have been brought up on natural foods before they became popular and before people began worrying that processed and refined foods might be making them sick. As a child, my mother used to make us fresh vegetable juice to drink when we got home from school. She also ordered organic grains from California which she would grind to make her own flour for bread. On a business trip to Hawaii, my father brought home a case of pineapples. In a typically Stark manner, those tops were planted in the front yard around a huge oak tree and, in time, supplied us and some of the neighborhood with fresh pineapples in an era when most people believed pineapples grew in cans.

As a child, I watched my grandmother swirl eggs in a blue and white speckled enamel fry-pan to make blintz shells without flour. From another grandmother, I learned what compote was. I learned to pickle a duck with garlic and to enhance a peach or cherry dish with almond. To this day, getting together in our family means getting together to share food and conversation.

When I was in my teens, the family orthodontist offered to tear up his bill and pay my mother fifty dollars per loaf for two loaves of her homemade seed bread. At this, my interest in food took a serious turn.

People say they'd like to eat natural foods, but can't afford them. However, if one compares nutrients, unit for unit, if one takes into account the greater health and well-being which real foods bring us, especially as we get older and our bodies start to wear down, the reduced visits to doctors and dentists, and the sheer pleasure one gets from eating good food, I believe that in the long run, natural foods turn out to be the better buy.

What are natural foods? Foods which have not been over-refined or treated with chemicals, and which do not contain harmful additives.

This book was written to share the fun we have with natural foods at our store! We feel lucky to be able to use food once considered exotic such as rices from Thailand, Greek feta cheese, or black turtle beans from South America as part of our daily preparation.

Not all recipes in this book are meant to be eaten regularly. There are dessert recipes which are high in fat content. But when you want to splurge, they are heavenly. Luscious and decadent can be natural too!

When we started this book, we had no idea there were so many people who can not eat dairy products or who become ill when they consume sugar or wheat. But we are learning from our customers and hope by the time our next book appears to be able to help people with allergies.

A whole food diet is not necessarily vegetarian. All the food groups are represented. For this reason, we have included poultry and fish.

Important Notes

All vegetables and fruits are washed before use. Organic whenever possible.

All dried beans are sorted for stones and rinsed before use.

Apart from onions and garlic, vegetables are not peeled unless specified. Vitamins and minerals lie just beneath the surface.

Eggs are large and free-range. In spite of the bad press, eggs are a wonderful food. They contain both unsaturated and saturated fats, are rich in lecithin, the cholesterol emulsifier, as well as choline, pyridoxine and inositol. They are also rich in vitamin A and are an excellent protein source.

Dishes baked in an oven are placed on the middle shelf.

Save liquid from steaming vegetables and cooking beans to use in soups, stew, etc. Stock is rich in nutrients and adds flavor.

Store nuts in the refrigerator or freezer. Their fat content causes nuts to become rancid if stored at room temperature.

Store grains in a cool, dry place. Heat and moisture are the main causes of deterioration.

Salt always means sea salt which is made from sun-evaporated seawater. Rich in minerals.

Baking powder should always be aluminum free. There are several brands available.

What You Need to Know

LEGUMES (peas and beans): Always sort and rinse before use to check for stones and debris. Refer to the chart below for cooking. Once cooked and cooled, legumes may be kept for several days in the refrigerator, or frozen. To freeze, cool, pack into jars and leave 1/2 inch at the top for expansion.

The amount of water used for cooking legumes is generally 3-4 times their volume, or to a level of 2" above beans, with more boiling water added as necessary during cooking.

LEGUMES (Dried Beans, Peas and Lentils)	SOAKING TIME	REGULAR COOKING TIME	PRESSURE COOKING TIME
Adzuki beans	3-4 hours	1 hour	15 minutes
Black-eyed peas	8-12 hours	1-1/2 hours	10-15 minutes
Black turtle beans	3-4 hours	1 hour	10-15 minutes
Cannellini beans	8-12 hours	1-1/2 hours	20 minutes
Ckickpeas	8-12 hours	3 hours	25 minutes
Kidney beans	8-12 hours	1-1/2 -2 hours	20 minutes
Lentils, brown	none	20 minutes	
Lentils, red	none	15 minutes	
Lima beans	4-8 hours	1-1/2 hours	20 minutes
Mung beans	4-8 hours	45 minutes	10 minutes
Navy beans	8-12 hours	1-1/2 hours	20 minutes
Pinto beans	8-12 hours	1-1/2 hours	20 minutes
Soybeans	8-12 hours	3 hours	50 minutes
Split peas, green	none	1-1-1/2 hours	
Split peas, yellow	none	1-1/2 hours	

Don't soak beans when using a pressure cooker. Nor is it necessary when cooking beans in a standard pot. Simply bring them to a boil uncovered, boil vigorously for 10 minutes to release the gases. Then, cover and simmer until soft.

Add salt or acidic ingredients, such as tomatoes, when legumes are almost finished cooking. Adding during cooking toughens them.

Legumes, stored away from sunlight and moisture, last for years. Beans excavated from Incan temples were capable of germination!

Substitute canned beans in any recipe. Drain and rinse first.

Usually 1 pound dry beans = 2 cups dry = 5-6 cups cooked.

GRAINS: Except for bulgur and couscous, grains are cooked by bringing the correct amount of cooking liquid to a boil in a pot large enough to accommodate the increase in volume after cooking. (Don't forget to use up that vegetable stock!) Add grain to boiling liquid, stir once, allow liquid to return to boiling, turn heat down low, cover pot and cook grains until they are soft. Do not stir grains after they come to a boil because too much stirring makes them gummy.

GRAIN	BOILING WATER to GRAIN	COOKING TIME
Amaranth	3 to 1	20-25 minutes
Barley, hulled	3 to 1	60-90 minutes
Barley, pearled	2 to 1	45 minutes
Buckwheat	2 to 1	15-20 minutes
Bulgur	1 to 1	pour boiling water over
Cornmeal	3 to 1	20-25 minutes
Couscous	1 to 1	pour boiling water over
Millet	2-1/2 to 1	25-30 minutes
Oats, rolled	2 to 1	20-30 minutes
Oats, steel cut	3 to 1	30 minutes
Quinoa	2 to 1	10 minutes
Rice, brown	2 to 1	45 minutes
Rice, wild	2 to 1	45-60 minutes

For hard grains, such as wheat, rye and barley, it is also possible to place them in a pot together with the water and bring them to a boil at the same time. Cook as above. Using this method for cooking rice makes it creamier.

Add salt to grains at the end because it slows the cooking process.

For bulgur and couscous, simply pour boiling water over the grain and stir once. Let grain sit for about 15-20 minutes, or until all the water is absorbed.

For fluffier grains, stir with a fork after grain is cooked and let sit, covered, in pot for an additional 10 minutes.

Should your rice be sticky, stir in several spoonfuls of soy granules. Allow pot to stand covered for 10 minutes. Not only will the granules absorb excess moisture, but they'll give rice a nutty flavor and gourmet look.

GRATING Pecorino Romano. A flavorful sheep's milk cheese tolerated well by many people who can't have dairy products. To grate: Using the steel blade of a food processor, place romano cut into 1-2 inch cubes in the workbowl. Grate about 2 cups at a time. Turn machine on and off several times and then let it run until cheese is grated. Grate more than you need for a particular recipe. Store extra in the refrigerator or freezer.

GREASING is done with a thin film of 1/2 soya liquid lecithin and 1/2 vegetable oil or butter. Liquid lecithin alone is too thick to spread easily. Diluting with oil works like magic. Always keep a jar of the lecithin-oil mixture on hand to grease with.

To grease, use a pastry brush to spread lecithin mixture. Natural grains tend to stick to pans, but will not when you use lecithin to grease.

OILS such as olive, sesame, and canola are flavorful. Because they are digested more slowly than other foods, oils help create a feeling of satiety.

SEEDS: Sesame seeds are always brown, unhulled, ones. Sunflower and pumpkin seeds are hulled.

No **SWEETENER** can be eaten with impunity and their use is often debated. We rely primarily upon honey or maple syrup for sweetening. Other options are fruit juice concentrate, rice syrup, barley malt, date sugar (made from dried pulverized dates), and a new discovery, the South American herb called Stevia.

TAHINI, sesame paste, is made from hulled toasted sesame seeds. Sesame butter uses unhulled sesame seeds. Use interchangeably. Both are wonderful sources of calcium and protein.

TAMARI and SHOYU soy sauces are fermented soy bean liquids which rise to the top when miso is made. Tamari and shoyu are processed without chemicals, unlike other soy sauces, and are rich in flavor. Tamari is wheat free, while shoyu is not.

OTHER UNFAMILIAR INGREDIENTS (available in most health food stores)

Fakin' Bacon is a tempeh (soy) vegetarian version of bacon that tastes amazingly like the real thing!

Nayonnaise is an egg-free tofu-based mayonnaise.

Sumac is a Middle Eastern spice.

Breakfasts

BREAKFAST

A bowl of hot cereal is a great way to start the morning. No recipe is needed. Simply cook up your favorite grain using four parts water to one part grain and cook until grain is soft. Some people like their grains chewy, others like them mushy. It's a matter of personal preference. When cooked, sprinkle grains with all kinds of things. Choose from among seeds, bran, raisins, or fruit. Use milk or soy milk. Or stir in a spoonful of honey or maple syrup. Sprinkle cereal with date sugar.

A light summer breakfast is yogurt with fresh fruit.

For those mornings when you make pancakes or waffles, use sour milk. When milk sours, don't pour it down the drain. Save in jars in the refrigerator. In the old days, milk was left in the cupboard to sour deliberately for use in pancakes and breads.

CORNMEAL-MOLASSES WAFFLES

Makes 12

Dark because of molasses, but light and crunchy due to cornmeal.

2 eggs
1 cup sour or buttermilk
1/4 cup safflower or canola
** oil**
1/4 cup Barbados molasses

1 cup cornmeal
1/3 cup whole wheat pastry
** flour**
1/2 teaspoon salt
2 teaspoons baking powder

Preheat and oil waffle iron using a pastry brush and a mixture of oil and liquid lecithin.

Blend all ingredients using a wire whisk or an electric blender.

Use 1/2 cup batter per waffle. Cook waffles until the light on the waffle iron goes out, signifying waffles are cooked. Serve at once with maple syrup or honey.

BLUEBERRY BUTTERMILK PANCAKES

Makes 6

For blueberry lovers! Best with wild blueberries. Great even with frozen, unsweetened berries.

1/2 cup whole wheat pastry flour	*1 teaspoon vanilla*
1 tablespoon toasted wheat germ	*1/4 teaspoon cinnamon*
1 tablespoon soy flour	*1 teaspoon baking powder*
3 eggs	□
1/2 cup sour or buttermilk, or	*1/2 cup blueberries*
soy milk	

Blend ingredients, except for blueberries, using a wire whisk, or the steel blade of a food processor and on/off turns. If using the processor, stop the machine once or twice to scrape down the sides of the workbowl with a rubber spatula.

Ladle pancake batter by 1/4 cupfuls onto hot, buttered griddle. Bake until bubbles form and begin to pop on the unbaked side. Press blueberries into the surface of pancakes and flip.

Bake pancakes until brown on the second side. Serve at once with maple syrup or honey.

PUMPKIN CORNCAKES

Makes 12

Leftover cooked sweet potatoes or squash can be substituted for pumpkin with equally delicious results.

1/2 cup cornmeal	**1 tablespoon honey**
1/2 cup cooked pumpkin	**1 cup boiling water**
1 cup whole wheat flour	**1 cup sweet, sour, or soy milk**
1/2 teaspoon salt	**2 teaspoons baking powder**
1 egg	

Blend all the ingredients using the steel blade of a food processor or an electric blender until the batter is smooth.

Ladle batter by 1/4 cupfuls onto hot, buttered griddle. Bake until bubbles form and begin to pop on the uncooked surface. Flip and brown on second side.

Serve hot with honey or maple syrup.

POPPY SEED CARDAMOM WAFFLES

Makes 12

Poppy seeds are a real treat. Cardamom, used in holiday baking, makes a special appearance and adds a heavenly fragrance.

1-1/3 cups sweet, sour, or soy milk	1-1/2 teaspoons baking powder
2 eggs	1/2 teaspoon salt
1/4 cup melted butter, safflower or canola oil	1/4 teaspoon cardamom
1/4 cup honey	1 tablespoon orange rind
1-1/4 cups whole wheat pastry flour	2 tablespoons poppy seeds

Preheat waffle iron; brush the grids with a mixture of liquid lecithin and oil or melted butter.

Blend all ingredients, except the poppy seeds, using the steel blade of a food processor and 10 quick on/off turns. Orange rind will be "grated." Add poppy seeds and scrape down the sides of the workbowl with a rubber spatula. Turn the food processor on and off quickly once or twice.

Bake waffles using 1/3 cup batter per waffle until signal light on waffle iron goes out, signifying waffles are ready to take out.

Top with honey or maple syrup and serve immediately.

DATE CORIANDER WAFFLES

Makes 12

Pour melted butter mixed with maple syrup or honey over date coriander waffles and watch them go!

1 cup sweet, sour, or soy milk	1/2 cup date sugar (or date
2 eggs	pieces rolled in oat flour)
1 cup whole wheat pastry flour	□
1/4 cup bran	1/3 cup melted butter
1 teaspoon baking powder	1/3 cup maple syrup or honey
1/4 teaspoon coriander	

Preheat waffle iron; brush the grids with a mixture of liquid lecithin and oil or melted butter.

Combine the ingredients (except melted butter and syrup or honey) using the steel blade of a food processor and 10 quick on/off turns.

Bake waffles using 1/3 cup batter per waffle until the signal light on the waffle iron goes out, signifying waffles are ready take out.

In the meantime, melt butter together with maple syrup.

Serve waffles with topping mixture drizzled on top.

MEXICAN CHILE WAFFLES

Makes 12

A spicy, filling way to start the day. Serve Mexican Chile Waffles as a weekend lunch or dinner.

1 pound cheddar cheese, or 1 pound soy cheese
1-1/3 cups sweet, sour, or soy milk
2 plum tomatoes
4 eggs

1 cup yellow cornmeal
2/3 cup whole wheat pastry flour
1 tablespoon baking powder
1 teaspoon chili powder
1/4 cup favorite salsa, medium or hot

Preheat waffle iron; brush grids with a mixture of liquid lecithin and melted butter or oil.

Grate cheddar cheese with the shredding disk of food processor using firm pressure. Remove grated cheese from work bowl.

Combine remaining ingredients using the steel blade and 10 quick on/off turns. Add cheese and mix in with 2 on/off turns.

Bake waffles using 1/3 cup batter per waffle until signal light on the waffle iron goes out, signifying waffles are ready to remove.

Serve immediately with extra salsa.

A good pepperjack cheese can be used if you like your food extra sharp and spicy!

OATMEAL GRIDDLE CAKES

Makes 12

Oatmeal on a griddle dressed up with molasses, honey or maple syrup.

1/2 cup whole wheat pastry flour
3 teaspoons baking powder
1 teaspoon salt
1 egg
1 tablespoon canola or
  safflower oil

1 tablespoon molasses or honey
1-1/2 cups sweet, sour, or soy
  milk
1-1/2 cups rolled oats

Preheat a buttered griddle.

Blend all the ingredients, except the oats, using a wire whisk or the steel blade of a food processor and 10 quick, on/off turns.

Add oats and incorporate with 2 quick on/off turns. Ladle 1/4 cup pancake batter per pancake onto griddle and cook until bubbles on uncooked side have popped. Flip and brown on second side.

Serve immediately with maple syrup or honey.

APPLE TOAST

Serves 4

Equally delicious with fresh peaches or apricots. Try mashing fresh berries to mix with honey and cinnamon.

**8 apples, peeled, cored and
    quartered
1/3 cup honey
1/2 teaspoon cinnamon**

**8 slices whole wheat bread
8 teaspoons butter**

Coarsely chop apples using the steel blade of a food processor. Place chopped apples in a pot together with honey and cinnamon. Cook for 5 minutes over medium high heat, until apples are fragrant and tender.

Toast the bread and place two slices per person on warm plates. Butter each slice with a teaspoon of butter and top with warm apple mixture.

Serve immediately with a glass of milk or cup of herbal tea.

CAROB-NUT GRANOLA

Makes 10 1/2 cup servings

Try carob-nut granola with a cup of herbal tea, a glass of milk or soy milk and serve for breakfast. This sweet, chewy "granola" is delicious and well-balanced. A real energy booster.

1 cup carob powder
3/4 cup toasted wheat germ
2 cups sunflower seeds
1 cup brown sesame seeds

1/4 cup wheat or oat bran
□
1/2 cup honey

Using the steel blade of the food processor, blend dry ingredients. With the machine running, add honey. Process until honey is incorporated and cereal resembles a streusel topping.

MOLASSES-MAPLE-NUTTY GRANOLA

Makes 12 servings

Dark and rich, high in iron.

1 cup maple syrup
1/2 cup blackstrap molasses
1/4 cup canola oil
□
4 teaspoons cinnamon

6 cups oats
1 cup walnut halves
2 cups pecan halves
2 cups pumpkin seeds
1/2 cup sunflower seeds

Preheat oven to 300 degrees.

Combine wet ingredients. Combine dry ingredients. (If you don't have a bowl large enough, divide ingredients between two bowls, for example, 5 cups oats in one bowl, and 5 cups oats in the second.) Pour wet ingredients over dry and mix well using your hands or a rubber spatula.

Divide granola between shallow baking pans and bake in a 300 degree oven until roasted and dry, about 1-1/2 hours. Stir every 15-20 minutes.

Let granola cool completely before storing in air-tight containers.

DEB'S GRANOLA

Makes 12 servings

For almond lovers - the best granola ever! Allergies? Feel free to substitute grains.

1/2 cup unsweetened coconut	1/4 cups wheat bran
3 cups sliced almonds	☐
2 cups rolled oats	1 cup maple syrup
1 cup wheat flakes	1/4 cup canola or safflower oil
1 cup rye flakes	1 teaspoon vanilla extract
1 cup barley flakes	1/4 teaspoon salt, optional

Preheat oven to 300 degrees.

Mix dry ingredients in a large bowl. (If you don't have a large enough bowl, divide dry ingredients between two, for example, 1 cup rolled oats in one bowl, and 1 cup oats in a second.) Pour wet ingredients over dry and mix well using your hands or a rubber spatula. Make sure all the grains are well-coated.

Spread granola in shallow pans and bake in the oven until golden brown and dry, about 1-1/2 hours. Stir every 15-20 minutes. Baking time varies due to weather, the size of your pans, your oven, etc.

When granola is dry and golden brown, remove from oven and stir. Let cool completely before storing in airtight containers.

SHASHOUKA

Serves 4

Of Greek origin, great for Sunday brunch.

1/4 cup olive oil
6 potatoes scrubbed, unpeeled
  and diced
1 red bell pepper, thinly sliced
1 green bell pepper, thinly sliced
2 onions, finely chopped
  □
2/3 cup tomato sauce

1 small dried chile pepper
1/2 teaspoon dried basil
1/2 teaspoon dried oregano
1/2 teaspoon salt
1/2 teaspoon black pepper
  □
8 eggs

In a large skillet, gently warm olive oil. Add potatoes, bell peppers and onions. Stir for 3 minutes. Add tomato sauce, herbs and spices, and cook another 3 minutes.

Reduce heat to low. Cover skillet and cook vegetables until tender, about 30 minutes. Stir several times during cooking to prevent sticking.

(Shashouka can be prepared up to this point one day in advance. Cool completely, cover, refrigerate. Reheat before continuing.)

Increase heat to medium-low. Break eggs on top of potato mixture. Cover and simmer about 3-4 minutes, or until eggs are set. Serve immediately.

Appetizers

APPETIZERS

Appetizers are those special foods one feeds family and friends while waiting for everyone to show up for dinner! They also make a light entree or good summer meal. There's always a bowl of houmous or black bean dip in our refrigerator and freezer for quick nibbles with fresh vegetables.

EGG ROLLS

Makes 8 egg rolls

Delicious vegetarian egg rolls without cornstarch. Cashews add a nutty flavor and prevent egg rolls from getting soggy.

1 package egg roll wrappers
□
1 pound soft tofu, mashed
2 cloves garlic, minced
1 cup bean sprouts
1/2 cup chopped water chestnuts
1/2 cup chopped bamboo shoots
1 cup Chinese cabbage,
   shredded, or bok choy, diced
1 cup pea pods, cut in thin strips

1/4 cup ground cashews
2 tablespoons tamari soy sauce
1/4 teaspoon ginger
pinch cayenne pepper
1/2 teaspoon black pepper
□
1 egg, lightly beaten
olive oil for sauteing, optional
egg white, optional

To prepare filling, mix together tofu, garlic, bean sprouts, water chestnuts, bamboo shoots, cabbage, pea pods, ground cashews, tamari, ginger and pepper.

Place 3/4 cup of filling diagonally on wrapper. Fold top corner down over filling. Fold side edges in and roll like a jellyroll. Seal rolls with beaten egg and set aside for about 15 minutes.

Egg rolls may be brushed with egg white and baked for 15 minutes at 350 degrees to save calories, or sauteed in a skillet in a little olive oil until nice and crisp and brown.

Egg rolls may be served with a homemade sweet and hot sauce: Blend 2 tablespoons prepared mustard with 1/2 cup frozen cranberries and a pinch of cayenne pepper.

NORI ROLLS

Serves 24

Dark, beautiful vegetarian sushi.

6 sheets toasted nori
□
2 cups raw Black Thai rice (a sticky rice)
4 cups water
□
1 package pickled sushi cucumbers, minced
1 package pickled sushi ginger, minced
1 tablespoon tahini

3 tablespoons tamari soy sauce
1 teaspoon black pepper
pinch cayenne pepper
□
2 carrots, grated
3 scallions, sliced
□
1 small jar pickled plum paste
□
Wasabi powder mixed with water to form paste

Bring water to a boil. Add rice, cover, lower heat, and simmer 45 minutes. Black Thai rice is sticky, which is perfect for this application. Allow rice to cool a little. When warm, mix with diced sushi cucumber, ginger, tahini, cayenne, black pepper, and soy sauce. Grate carrots and slice scallions, and set aside.

Place a dish of water on the work counter to moisten hands while working. Place a sheet of nori on work surface and lightly brush with pickled plum paste. Place 1/2 cup rice mixture on nori. Wet hands and pat rice to cover nori from side to side, leaving 1" at the top and 2" at the bottom. Sprinkle scallion and carrots near the bottom edge of the rice and roll the seaweed into a cigar-shaped cylinder. Cylinder should be firm and well-filled. Dampen outer edge of nori so it will stick when rolled.

When all sheets of nori are filled, slice each cylinder in 2" rounds using a sharp, wet knife. Arrange on a platter and serve with wasabi sauce for dipping.

ESCABECHE

Serves 12

Escabeche makes a great appetizer or main dish. Marinate overnight before serving. Escabeche keeps in the refrigerator for up to three weeks and improves with age!

1/2 cup fragrant green olive oil
2 pounds shelled and deveined
  shrimp (20-24 per pound)
  □
2 large onions, quartered
  and thinly sliced
6 cloves garlic, minced
2 medium carrots, halved and
  thinly sliced

2/3 cup apple cider or wine
  vinegar
2 bay leaves
1 teaspoon salt
1 teaspoon black pepper
1 teaspoon paprika

Gently warm olive oil in a large skillet and saute shrimp for two minutes, just until they turn pink. Transfer shrimp to a bowl.

Using the same skillet, saute onions, garlic and carrots for 5 minutes. Add vinegar, bay leaves, salt, pepper and paprika. Stir and cook for 2 minutes.

Pour vegetables with marinade over shrimp and mix lightly.

Cover and chill overnight.

VEGETABLE PATE

Makes two pates, each to serve 12　　　　　　*Bake at 350*

A glorious pate, tender, without cream or butter. There are two distinct layers. Garnish with sweet red pepper strips and a sprig of watercress or parsley. This pate freezes well.

First Layer
- 2 tablespoons olive oil
- 1-1/2 pounds zucchini
- 1 bunch scallions
- 3 cloves garlic, minced
- 1 pound spinach
- □

- 2 eggs
- 1/2 teaspoon tarragon
- 1/2 teaspoon dried dill weed
- 1/4 teaspoon cayenne
- 1 tsp each salt and pepper
- 1 cup dry whole wheat bread crumbs

Second Layer
- 2 tablespoons olive oil
- 1/2 cup minced onion
- 2 cloves garlic, minced
- □
- 1 pound grated carrot
- 2 cups cooked potatoes

- 2 eggs
- 1/2 teaspoon thyme
- 1-1/2 teaspoons tarragon
- 1 teaspoon each salt and black pepper
- 1 cup dry whole wheat bread crumbs

For first layer, gently warm olive oil and saute vegetables until tender. Drain liquid. Using the steel blade of a food processor, blend vegetables with eggs, seasonings and bread crumbs.

Fill 2 greased 6-cup bread pans half full.

Proceed in the same way for the second layer, this time adding cooked potatoes to the processor.

Cover first layer with second and tap pans on counter to remove air bubbles. Lightly cover pans with foil and place in a larger pan in the oven. Fill larger pan with water 2/3 way up the sides of bread pans. Bake 1-1/2 hours at 350, or until knife inserted into the center of the pate comes out clean.

Cool in oven. Remove bread pans from large pan. Refrigerate pates for two days. For a more compact pate, stack pans. After a day, switch pans.

To unmold, run a knife around the outside of the pate and turn onto a platter. If there is difficulty removing the pates, run the knife around again and smack the bottom of the pan smartly.

HOMEMADE MARINATED SUN-DRIED TOMATOES

Makes 3 cups

Delicious on pasta, rice or beans. Try sun-dried tomatoes on French bread as an appetizer.

6 ounces sun-dried tomatoes
1-1/2 cups apple cider vinegar
☐
1-1/3 cups olive oil
18 cloves garlic, sliced
12 whole black peppercorns

2 teaspoons dried basil
1 teaspoon dried oregano
1/2 teaspoon dried tarragon
1/2 teaspoon dried thyme
1/2 teaspoon dried marjoram
1 teaspoon dried parsley

Place tomatoes in a non-plastic or non-aluminum bowl. Heat vinegar in a stainless steel pot. Pour over tomatoes and let sit for 1 hour, stirring occasionally.

Drain tomatoes (save vinegar for use elsewhere).

Combine remaining ingredients in a large glass jar. Add tomatoes, stir and cover. Let tomatoes marinate for at least 24 hours.

Marinated tomatoes keep for several months. They may be stored for a longer period in the refrigerator, but bring to room temperature before serving.

DEBRA'S SALSA

Makes about 7 cups

A chunky and highly seasoned salsa, especially good on tacos or with chips. Try it on beans, fish, chicken or burritos.

2 large onions, chopped
2 cloves garlic, chopped
1 jalapeno pepper, seeded and
  minced
4 cups tomatoes, diced
1 cup tomato puree
1 cup water
1/2 tablespoon chili powder

1 teaspoon cumin
1/2 teaspoon salt, optional
1/2 teaspoon black pepper
1/4 teaspoon celery seed,
  optional
1/4 teaspoon basil
1/4 teaspoon oregano
2 tablespoons chopped parsley

Combine all the ingredients in a large stainless steel or enamel soup pot and simmer for 10 minutes.

This salsa keeps for several weeks when refrigerated.

PUMPKIN SEED-TOMATILLO DIP

Makes about 4 cups

A terrific party dip for tortilla chips, or a refreshing and low-calorie sauce for rice, beans, chicken or fish.

2 cups tomatillos, husked
□
1 cup pumpkin seeds
□
4 large garlic cloves
1/2 teaspoon dried coriander
2 jalapeno peppers, seeded
1/4 cup fresh parsley
2-1/2 tablespoons fresh lime
   juice

1/2 cup water
1 teaspoon salt
1 teaspoon black pepper
□
few tablespoons olive oil,
   optional
minced red onion as garnish

Place husked tomatillos in a pot with enough water to cover; bring to a boil, cook for 2 minutes and then drain.

Roast pumpkin seeds in a 350 degree oven on a cookie sheet for 4 minutes, until lightly toasted and fragrant, but still green. Cool.

Using the steel blade of a food processor and on/off turns, puree tomatillos, pumpkin seeds, garlic, coriander, jalapeno peppers, parsley, lime juice, water, salt and pepper. If desired, add a few tablespoons of olive oil.

Refrigerate if not using immediately. Dip keeps for a week in the refrigerator.

BLACK BEAN DIP

Makes about 8 cups

Similar to guacamole, without fat, black bean dip is a real crowd pleaser! Serve it with your favorite corn chips or strips of sweet red pepper, jicama, and celery sticks.

8 cups cooked black beans and
    enough liquid to blend,
    about 2 cups
2-3 teaspoons salt
1/2 teaspoon dried coriander
1/4 teaspoon cayenne

3 jalapeno peppers, seeded
1 cup salsa, hot, med. or mild
1/4 cup lime juice
1/4 cup lemon juice
3 cloves garlic

Using the steel blade of a food processor, blend all the ingredients until the beans are fairly smooth, adding cooking liquid (up to 2 cups) as needed, to reach desired consistency. Don't overblend. We like some pieces of black bean to remain for aesthetic reasons.

Store black bean dip in the refrigerator, but serve at room temperature.

Black bean dip keeps two weeks refrigerated and also freezes well.

MARINATED MUSHROOMS

Makes about 8 cups

Quick and easy to make. Once the mushrooms are removed from the marinade, use to pickle more mushrooms or other vegetables such as zucchini spears.

2 pounds small mushrooms, cleaned and trimmed	**1 large onion, quartered**
	1 tablespoon oregano
□	**1 teaspoon salt**
1 cup cider vinegar	**1 teaspoon black pepper**
3 cloves garlic	**1 cup olive oil**

Place mushrooms in a glass, ceramic, or stainless-steel bowl.

Using the steel blade of a food processor or a blender, blend garlic and onion with vinegar. Add blended mixture to mushrooms together with oregano, salt, pepper and olive oil.

Cover tightly and refrigerate overnight. Stir once or twice to make sure that the top mushrooms get turned under.

Remove mushrooms from the marinade with a slotted spoon. Delicious in tossed salads or serve as an appetizer.

HOUMOUS BI TAHINI

Makes 6 cups

Probably the best-known and best-loved Mid-East dish is houmous. Full of protein, calcium, fiber, and high in carbohydrates. Eat with pita and raw vegetables - what a meal!

4 cups cooked or canned chickpeas
1 cup tahini (sesame butter)
1 cup liquid from beans

1/2 cup lemon juice
5 cloves garlic
1-1/2 teaspoons salt
dash cayenne pepper

Puree all ingredients using the steel blade of a food processor until the mixture moves freely under the blade and the garlic is well-incorporated. Add more liquid from beans if the mixture seems too stiff. Stop machine once or twice to scrape down the sides of the workbowl with a rubber spatula.

Cover and refrigerate houmous for several hours to give the flavors a chance to blend. Serve at room temperature.

Houmous keeps in the refrigerator for about a week. Store in the freezer for longer periods.

STUFFED GRAPE LEAVES

Makes 36

Heavenly! The stuffing is wonderful in swiss chard or cabbage leaves too.

1 jar vine leaves (or about 36 fresh vine leaves, steamed until they turn a light green)
☐
4 tablespoons olive oil
2 medium onions, chopped
2 cloves garlic, minced
1 tablespoon dried parsley
☐
1 teaspoon dried dill weed
1 teaspoon dried mint

1 cup raw rice (use Thai red, Wehani, or short-grain brown)
1/2 cup pine nuts (or chopped walnuts)
1/2 teaspoon salt
1/2 teaspoon black pepper
1/4 cup lemon juice
1-1/2 cups water
☐
1/4 cup lemon juice
3/4 cup olive oil

Remove vine leaves from jar and rinse with hot water in a colander. Drain well. Pat leaves dry. Place on linen towels with shiny side down.

Gently warm 4 tablespoons olive oil in a skillet. Saute onion, garlic, and parsley until onion is soft, about 2-3 minutes. Add dill, mint, rice and pine nuts. Saute 5 minutes. Rice will become fragrant. Add salt and pepper, 1/4 cup lemon juice, and the water. Cover and simmer for 40 minutes.

Cool rice mixture. When cool, place 2 teaspoons pilaf in the middle of the underside (not the shiny side) of the leaf near the stem. Roll grape leaves up egg-roll style by folding over the base side of the leaf (where the stem is attached), and folding in the sides. Roll tightly away from you.

Arrange grape leaves in layers in an oven proof pot which has a heavy lid. Sprinkle each layer with a mixture of the remaining 1/4 cup lemon juice and 3/4 cup olive oil.

Weight the stuffed grape leaves with a plate. Cover. Bake in an 350 degree oven for 1/2 hour. When done baking, drain leaves and refrigerate. (Save oil and lemon mixture to use over other grains.) Serve grape leaves cold.

Some people like their grape leaves with yogurt.

If fresh leaves are used, you may want to increase the quantity of salt in the stuffing by 1/2 teaspoon.

Grape leaves store well in the refrigerator for about a week.

CHEESE AND GREEN CHILE DIP

Makes about 7 cups

What doesn't taste luscious with melted cheese? Cheese and Green Chile Dip works equally well with soy cheese. Nutritional information is based upon dairy cheese. Soy cheese is somewhat lower in fat and has no cholesterol.

tortilla chips
□
2 large white onions, minced
2 large tomatoes, chopped

1 can (4 ounces) green chiles, minced
□
1 pound cheddar or Monterey Jack cheese, grated

Place tortilla chips on cookie sheets in the oven to warm.

Place chopped onions, tomato and green chiles in a frying pan. Simmer for 5 minutes over a low heat. Add cheese and cook gently for another five minutes.

Serve dip with warm tortilla chips.

BABAGANOUSH

Makes about 4 cups

Loved throughout the Middle East, babaganoush is served with pita or vegetables, garnished with spicy black olives and a little paprika sprinkled on top.

2 large eggplants	**1/4 teaspoon cumin**
□	**2/3 cup sesame tahini**
4 cloves garlic	**1/4 cup lemon juice**
1/2 teaspoon salt	**pinch cayenne pepper**
	paprika to garnish

Prick eggplants with knife so they won't explode in the oven. Bake on a cookie sheet until the eggplant meat feels soft. Cool slightly and then scrape eggplant out of skin and place in the workbowl of a food processor. (Instead of baking eggplants, they may also be steamed in a pot with water until soft.)

Using the steel blade of a food processor, blend eggplant meat with garlic, salt, cumin, tahini and lemon juice until desired smoothness has been achieved.

Spoon babaganoush into a bowl and serve at room temperature. Store in the refrigerator for up to 2 weeks. If desired, freeze.

PICKLED FISH WITH CHILE PEPPERS

Serves 6

Marinate this spicy appetizer for 24 hours before serving. Any firm white fish fillets work well.

2 pounds fish fillets, cut into
   1-1/2 inch cubes
3 tablespoons lemon juice
   □
2 tablespoons olive oil
   □
2 tablespoons olive oil
1 large onion, minced
1 carrot, thinly sliced
1 teaspoon salt
1 teaspoon curry
1/4 teaspoon ginger

2 cloves garlic, chopped
1/4 teaspoon coriander
1/8 teaspoon cumin
4 whole peppercorns
3/4 cup cider vinegar
1/2 cup water
3 bay leaves
1 dried jalapeno or other hot
   chile pepper
   □
leafy lettuce to bed plates
lemon slices and watercress for
   garnish

Place fish in glass dish. Sprinkle lemon juice over it, cover, and chill for several hours, turning once or twice.

Remove fish from dish and place on rack to air dry for 20 minutes. Gently warm oil in heavy skillet. Add fish in batches (do not crowd) and cook until opaque, stirring occasionally, about 2 minutes. Transfer cooked fish to clean glass bowl.

Warm remaining oil in clean skillet. Add onions and carrot and cook until soft, about 5 minutes. Reduce heat to low and add salt, curry, ginger, chopped garlic, coriander, cumin, and peppercorns. Stir until fragrant, about 2 minutes. Mix in vinegar, water, bay leaves, and chile. Increase heat and simmer 5 minutes to blend flavors.

Pour mixture over fish. Cover and refrigerate for 24 hours.

Before serving, remove fish from the refrigerator and let stand at room temperature for 20 minutes.

Serve on a lettuce leaf garnished with lemon slices and watercress.

This dish also works well with tofu instead of fish.

MINTED EGGPLANT

Serves 4-6

A savory appetizer with crackers or pita.

1 eggplant, peeled and cubed	**1/2 teaspoon cumin**
1/2 cup olive oil	**1/4 teaspoon cayenne pepper**
□	□
2 cups plain low-fat yogurt	**salt and black pepper to taste**
1 large clove garlic, pressed	**fresh mint leaves or sprigs of**
1 teaspoon dried mint leaves	**parsley for garnish**

Preheat oven to 450 degrees.

Toss eggplant cubes with olive oil. Bake on a cookie sheet in the oven, turning pieces once, until eggplant is tender and lightly browned, about 15-20 minutes.

In a bowl, combine yogurt, garlic, dried mint, cumin and cayenne pepper. Fold warm eggplant into yogurt mixture. Cover and refrigerate for 24 hours, stirring several times.

Remove from the refrigerator 1-2 hours before serving so that the eggplant will be cool, not cold. Stir well, taste, add salt and pepper if desired, and garnish with mint leaves or parsley.

WHITE BEAN ROASTED GARLIC GREMOLATA

Makes 1-1/2 cups

A simplified gremolata. Serve with endive, radicchio leaves, carrot, fennel sticks and snow peas.

2 cups cooked cannellini (white kidney) beans
1/4 cup lemon juice
1 tablespoon olive oil
6 cloves garlic

1/3 cup packed Italian flat parsley
1/2 teaspoon salt
1 teaspoon black pepper

Using the steel blade of a food processor, blend everything until smooth.

Transfer dip to a serving bowl and place vegetables around it.

Although this dip can be prepared a day ahead and refrigerated, bring to room temperature before serving.

SMOKED SALMON MOUSSE

Makes 1-1/2 cups

Pipe this onto cucumber or pumpernickel rounds. Garnish with sprigs of fresh dill.

8 ounces natural cream cheese, room temperature
1/2 cup nonfat yogurt
4 ounces smoked salmon
1 tablespoon lemon juice
1 teaspoon dried dill weed

1/2 teaspoon black pepper
□
4 scallions, sliced, green and white parts
small sprigs of fresh dill

Blend cream cheese, yogurt, smoked salmon, lemon juice, dill weed and black pepper. Transfer to a bowl and stir in sliced scallions.

May also be used as a spread or dip.

Breads

BREADS

There's nothing like the aroma of fresh bread baking in the oven! Here are some helpful hints.

Have ingredients at room temperature before mixing.

Liquid in which yeast is dissolved must be lukewarm, comfortable to the touch. Yeast can be killed by temperatures that are too high or too low.

A teaspoon of sweetener activates yeast. Yeast should become foamy when mixed with water and a natural sugar in 10 minutes. If not, start over. Either the water temperature is too hot or too cold, or your yeast is bad.

Store dry baking yeast in the freezer in an air-tight container where it will keep forever.

To rise, dough must be warm and kept in a draft-free location. Plastic wrap or a shower cap keeps the dough warm and keeps out drafts. When you cover the dough with a towel, be careful not to place where there is a draft.

Greasing with lecithin keeps whole grains from sticking.

Baked goods dry out in the refrigerator. Store in the freezer.

Bake breads the amount of time specified, then check to see if done by tapping on the bottom. Bread should sound hollow.

Save soured milk for use in muffins. Nothing makes them rise better. There will be no hint of sourness in the final product.

CRACKLING CORN BREAD

Serves 6   *Bake at 450*

Coarse cornmeal or corn grits give this bread extra crackle. Great with soups or chili.

1 cup coarse cornmeal
  or corn grits
1/2 teaspoon salt
1/2 teaspoon baking powder

1 cup sour milk or yogurt
1 egg
1 teaspoon dried rosemary
2 teaspoons olive oil

Preheat oven to 450 degrees.

Grease a 9-inch square cookie pan.

Combine cornmeal, salt and baking powder.

In a small bowl, beat together sour milk, egg, rosemary and olive oil. Pour sour milk mixture over cornmeal and stir until smooth. Do not over mix.

Spoon batter into pan. Shake pan slightly to spread batter evenly. Bake corn bread until set and a knife inserted into the center comes out clean, about 15 minutes.

When baked, cool corn bread 5 minutes in pan. Cut into six portions and serve warm.

ADAM'S FAVORITE CORN BREAD

Serves 6   *Bake at 375*

My son, Adam, used to ask for this corn bread whenever soup was on and there was company for dinner.

1 cup coarse yellow cornmeal
1/4 cup soy or brown rice flour
1/4 cup whole wheat flour
2 teaspoons baking powder

1 teaspoon salt
2 eggs
1 cup sweet or sour milk
*1 tablespoon honey or rice
   syrup*

Preheat oven to 375 degrees.

Grease a 9-inch pan.

In a bowl, mix dry ingredients together. In a second bowl, combine wet ingredients. Pour wet ingredients over dry and stir with a wooden spoon. Pour batter into pan and bake corn bread 30 minutes, or until lightly browned around the edges.

Remove from the oven and cool corn bread 5 minutes in the pan. Cut into six pieces while still warm and serve with butter. Corn bread also freezes well.

SHERRY'S AUNT DOLLY'S RYE BREAD

Makes 2 loaves   *Bake at 350*

Real Jewish Rye Bread!

2 cups warm water	**1 tablespoon vinegar**
1 tablespoon baking yeast	**1 tablespoon caraway seeds**
1 tablespoon malt or honey	**2 cups rye flour**
☐	**☐**
1 tablespoon salt	**approx 3-1/2 cups unbleached flour**

Mix yeast, malt and water. Let sit for 10 minutes until mixture bubbles. Add salt, vinegar, caraway seeds and rye flour. Add enough white flour to make a soft, not sticky dough.

Turn dough out onto a board and knead for 10 minutes, adding more flour if necessary to keep the dough from sticking.

Form dough into a ball. Place in a bowl and cover with a towel. Let rise in a draft-free spot until doubled in bulk, about 1-2 hours. Shape into two loaves. Make a few slashes on the tops with a sharp knife. Sprinkle a cookie sheet with cornmeal. Put the loaves on it and let rise about 1/2 hour.

Bake at 350 degrees for about 50 minutes, or until the loaves sound hollow when tapped on the bottom.

MOM'S BREAD

Makes 28 flat breads   *Bake at 350*

In 1962, our family dentist tore up his bill for $100 in exchange for 2 loaves of mom's bread. It's survival food! We make mom's bread in cookie form, which is easier to serve and eat.

1 teaspoon honey or barley malt	1/3 cup rye flakes
1 teaspoon molasses	1/3 cup soy flakes
2/3 cup warm water	1/3 cup cornmeal
2 tablespoons baking yeast	1/3 cup seven-grain cereal
□	2 tablespoons caraway seeds
3 cups w/w bread flour	1 teaspoon sea salt
□	1/3 cup wheat, rice or oat
1/2 cup barley flakes	bran
1/2 cup wheat flakes	1/3 cup pumpkin seeds
1/2 cup rolled oats	1/3 cup sunflower seeds
1/3 cup rice flakes	1/3 cup sesame seeds
1/3 cup flax seeds	□
1/3 cup millet	2-3 cups warm water

Grains and flours should be at room temperature.

Pour 2/3 cup hot water over sweeteners in a large jar or bowl. When water cools to lukewarm, add yeast and stir to dissolve. Place mixture in a warm, draft-free location until the mixture is foamy.

Place flour in large mixing bowl. Using the steel blade of a food processor, blend all grains, flakes and seeds. Some grains, like millet, will remain almost whole, so don't expect the mixture to be smooth. Add grains to flour in bowl and mix. Then add yeast mixture. Gradually stir in 2-3 glasses of warm water, just enough so dough will hold together.

Grease baking sheets. Place mom's bread, roughly 1/3 cup dough per bread, on baking sheets about 3-inches apart to allow room for rising. Flatten each slightly with the palm of the hand. If using an electric oven, warm to 200 degrees and turn off before putting breads in to rise for 15 minutes. If using gas, put baking sheets in a turned off oven and let breads rise for the same amount of time.

When batter has risen, turn oven to 350 degrees and bake until rolls are lightly browned, about 30 minutes. Remove to cooling racks.

We like to toast mom's bread until nice and brown. However, when cool, it is like hard-tack, great to take hiking or on vacations because it will not mold.

CHALLAH

Makes 2 large loaves   *Bake at 400*

Traditional Friday night challah, braided, golden, makes a
beautiful centerpiece.

pinch saffron	**1/4 cup canola oil**
2 cups hot water	**3 tablespoons honey**
□	□
8 cups unbleached flour	**4 eggs**
1-1/2 teaspoons salt	**1 tablespoon canola oil**
2 tablespoons baking yeast	**poppy seeds**

Dissolve saffron in hot water. Cool until lukewarm.

Using the dough hook of an electric mixer on low speed,
combine 1-1/2 cups flour, salt, yeast, oil and honey. Add warm
saffron-water and mix. Add 3 eggs (save 4th egg for later), one
at a time, beating well after each. Add remaining flour, 1/2 cup
at a time. Knead challah with mixer for 5 minutes.

Place 1 tablespoon oil in a bowl. Place dough inside bowl
and turn to coat. Cover bowl with plastic wrap and place in a
warm place to rise until double, about an hour.

Punch dough down. Turn out onto bread board and knead
several minutes. Divide dough in half. Divide each half into
quarters. For each loaf, roll three pieces of dough into ropes
about 15" long. Braid the three pieces together. The 4th piece
of dough for each loaf is also divided into 3 pieces and braided
to form a small loaf which is placed decoratively on top of the
larger bread.

Place challah on greased cookie sheet and cover with a clean cloth. Allow to rise until double, about 20 minutes.

While bread rises, preheat oven to 400 degrees. When risen, brush loaves with reserved egg mixed with a little water. Sprinkle with poppy seeds.

Bake 25 minutes, or until hollow when thumped on bottom. Allow to cool on rack.

Challah is most delicious the day it is made.

AMY'S WHOLE WHEAT "QUICK" FRENCH BREAD

Makes 1 loaf   *Bake at 400*

Only an hour and a half from inception to ingestion! Use a pocket thermometer to measure the water temperature for best results.

> **3 cups whole wheat bread flour**   **1-1/4 cups hot (120 degrees)**
> **1 teaspoon salt**   **water**
> **1 tablespoon baking yeast**   **1 tablespoon honey**

Using the steel blade of a food processor, place flour and salt in workbowl. Dissolve honey and yeast in water, and let yeast proof until it starts to bubble, usually 5 minutes.

Turn on the food processor and pour yeast mixture through feed tube. Process just until dough forms a ball, and then 30 seconds more. Dough will be slightly sticky and soft.

Leave dough in workbowl, or if workbowl is needed, let dough rise covered in another ungreased bowl. Providing water temperature is hot (120 degrees), but not too hot (128 degrees), dough will double in bulk in about 20 minutes.

When dough has doubled, turn onto bread board and knead lightly by hand, adding extra flour only if necessary to handle.

Form loaf of french bread, place on a greased cookie sheet, cover, and let rise another 20 minutes. While bread rises a second time, preheat oven to 400 degrees. Then bake 35 minutes. Eat and enjoy!

7-GRAIN CEREAL BREAD

Makes 1 loaf   *Bake at 400*

1 tablespoon baking yeast   **1/2 teaspoon salt**
1 tablespoon honey   **2 tablespoons flax seeds**
1-1/4 cups warm water or milk   **2 tablespoons brewer's yeast**
    □   **(optional)**
3 cups whole wheat flour   **1/4 cup olive or sesame oil**
1/2 cup 7-grain cereal   **2 tablespoons cider vinegar**

Using the steel blade of a food processor, combine yeast, honey and warm water. Let stand for 15 minutes until frothy.

Add the remaining ingredients and knead with the steel blade until the dough cleans the sides of the workbowl and appears smooth and pliable. If dough appears too dry, add water, 1 tablespoon at a time. If it appears too sticky, add 1 tablespoon of flour at a time.

Place dough in a bowl with 1 tablespoon oil and turn to coat. Cover with plastic wrap, or a shower cap, and let rise until doubled in bulk, about 50 minutes.

Grease bread pan. Punch down dough. Shape and put in pan. Cover and let bread rise again for another 50 minutes.

Preheat oven to 400 degrees. When bread is risen, bake 40 minutes, or until lightly browned. If bread sounds hollow when thumped on bottom, it's done.

Place bread pan on rack to cool for 10 minutes. Turn bread out from pan to finish cooling before slicing.

PEPPERY BREAD WREATH

Makes 1 bread wreath   *Bake at 350*

1 tablespoon baking yeast   **1 tablespoon black pepper**
1-1/2 cups warm water   **1 tablespoon dried rosemary**
              □   **1/4 cup brown sesame seeds**
2-1/2 cups w/w pastry flour   **1/4 cup poppy seeds**
1 cup w/w bread flour   □
1/4 cup olive oil   **1 egg yolk beaten with**
1 teaspoon salt   **milk or water as a glaze**

Sprinkle yeast over warm water in the workbowl of a food processor. Using the steel blade, stir to dissolve. Let stand 10 minutes until foamy.

To the workbowl, add flours, olive oil, salt, black pepper, rosemary, and half the sesame and poppy seeds. Knead for a minute with on/off turns, until dough cleans the sides of the workbowl and appears smooth and elastic. Add a tablespoon more flour if dough appears too sticky; add a tablespoon water if it appears too dry. Don't overprocess as the heat of the motor will kill the yeast.

Pour 2 tablespoons olive oil into a large bowl. Add dough, turning to coat. Cover bowl with plastic wrap, or a shower cap, and let dough rise until doubled in bulk, about 1 hour.

Grease a cookie sheet. Punch down dough. Cut into 8 pieces. Form each into a ball and roll in remaining sesame and poppy seeds. Arrange balls in a ring on the cookie sheet, flattening slightly so they touch and form a wreath. Cover with a towel and place in a warm draft-free spot. Let rise until doubled in bulk again, about 35 minutes.

Preheat oven to 350 degrees.

Bake wreath 20 minutes. Brush with egg yolk and water as glaze and continue baking until bread is golden and sounds hollow when tapped on bottom, about 10 minutes.

Remove bread from oven and cool on rack.

Best served the same day it is made. The pepper in this bread gives it a little unexpected kick.

THREE-GRAIN WILD RICE BREAD

Makes 1 large loaf or 12 rolls   *Bake at 375*

Serve with bowls of hearty bean soup and a green salad. Wild rice gives a wonderful look and texture to this bread and it gets crunchy as it bakes.

1 tablespoon baking yeast	1/2 cup yellow cornmeal
1/3 cup warm water	1/2 cup rolled oats
□	□
2 cups sour or soy milk	4-1/2 cups w/w flour
1/4 cup honey or rice syrup	□
1/4 cup molasses or malt syrup	1 cup cooked wild
2 tablespoons olive oil	rice
2 teaspoons salt	
2 cups w/w pastry flour or spelt flour	

Sprinkle yeast over warm water in the workbowl of a food processor. Using the steel blade, turn the machine on and off twice to dissolve yeast. Let stand 5 minutes until foamy. Stir in milk, honey, molasses, oil, salt, whole wheat pastry flour, cornmeal and oats with on/off turns. Add two cups bread flour and knead in using on/off turns, about 20 seconds. Do not overprocess. The heat from the motor will kill the yeast.

Remove dough to lightly floured surface and cover. Let rest 15 minutes.

By hand, knead in remaining bread flour, 1/2 cup at a time, and cooked wild rice. Dough will be stiff. Add 2 tablespoons olive oil to a bowl and add dough, turning to coat. Cover and let rise in a warm draft-free place until doubled in volume, about 1 hour.

Punch dough down. Turn onto bread board. Knead until smooth. If making rolls, divide dough into 12 pieces. Roll each piece into a ball. Arrange balls on the baking sheet. If making a loaf of bread, either place dough in bread pan, or shape and place on a cookie sheet. Let bread or rolls rise in warm draft-free place until almost doubled, about 45 minutes.

While bread rises, preheat oven to 375 degrees. Bake 45 minutes, or until hollow when tapped on bottom. If making rolls, bake 30 minutes. When bread is baked, cool 10 minutes in the pan (if using one) on a rack. Then turn out to finish cooling.

HERB BREAD

Makes 1 loaf   *Bake at 350*

1/2 cup scalded milk	1 egg
2 tablespoons butter or olive oil	1/2 teaspoon basil
1 tablespoon honey	1/2 teaspoon thyme
1-1/2 teaspoons salt	1 teaspoon oregano
1/2 cup water	2 teaspoons chives
1 tablespoon baking yeast	3-1/4 cups w/w flour

Scald milk by bringing to a boil. When skin forms on top, combine milk with butter, honey and salt in a food processor using the steel blade. Cool to lukewarm by adding the water. Add yeast and mix with several on/off turns. Add egg, herbs and flour. Mix with several on/off turns. When dough forms a ball and cleans the workbowl, divide it into 7 or 8 smaller balls, press them around the blade, and process again for a second or two. Repeat this process twice.

Pour 1 tablespoon olive oil in bowl. Add dough, turning to coat, cover, and let rise until doubled in bulk, about 45 minutes. Punch down, shape dough into a loaf, place in a greased bread pan and let rise, covered, until double in bulk again, about 1 hour.

While bread rises, preheat oven to 350 degrees. Bake one hour.

When bread is baked, let stand in pan on rack for 10 minutes. Turn out on rack to finish cooling.

BASIC MUFFIN RECIPE

Makes 12 meal-size muffins, or 18 large   Bake at 375

Using the basic recipe, vary the fruits to your heart's content. When using blueberries, substitute 1 teaspoon nutmeg for cinnamon. When using poppy seeds, add some grated lemon peel.

1/2 pound soft tofu
3 large ripe or frozen bananas
3 eggs
1/2 cup sweetener (honey, fruit
   concentrate, or maple syrup)
2 teaspoons vanilla
1/2 cup sour or soy milk
   □
3-1/2 cups w/w pastry flour
1 cup oats

4 teaspoons baking powder
1 teaspoon baking soda
2 teaspoons cinnamon
1/4 teaspoon salt
   □
2 cups cranberries, blueberries,
   cut-up pears, peaches,
   apples, raisins, date
   pieces or poppy seeds

Preheat oven to 375 degrees.   Grease muffin tins.

Blend first six ingredients in a food processor until no pieces of tofu or banana remain.

Mix dry ingredients in a large bowl.   Combine wet and dry ingredients and mix briefly to moisten.   Using a rubber spatula, stir in fruit or poppy seeds.   Using a 1/3 cup measure, spoon batter into 12 muffin wells.

Bake 25 minutes.   Muffins will be light brown.   When baked, cool muffins for 10 minutes in tins on racks; then turn out on racks to finish cooling.

BEATRICE'S BASIC MUFFIN RECIPE

Makes 12 muffins   *Bake at 350*

These muffins contain no baking powder. Baking powder is high in sodium and destroys some B-vitamins.

4 eggs whites (yolks are in Group 3)

Group 1
> **1 cup sifted w/w pastry flour**
> **1/3 cup each wheat germ, bran and rolled oats**
> **1/4 cup powdered milk, optional**
> **pinch salt, optional**
> **pinch nutmeg or allspice, optional**
> **1/2 teaspoon cinnamon**

Group 2
> **1/2 cup raisins or chopped dates or other dried fruit**
> **1/2 cup chopped walnuts or pecans**

Group 3
> **1/2 cup yogurt or buttermilk**
> **1/2 cup apple juice**
> **1/2 cup applesauce or one banana or 1/2 cup grated carrot**
> **1/4 cup honey or molasses**
> **1 teaspoon vanilla**
> **4 egg yolks**

Using an electric mixer or hand beater, beat egg whites until stiff. Set aside.

Mix Group 1 ingredients in a large bowl. Place ingredients from Group 3 in blender and blend thoroughly. Stir liquid ingredients into dry.

Stir in Group 2 raisins (dates) and walnuts (pecans).

Fold in egg whites quickly using a rubber spatula.

Spoon muffin batter into 12 previously greased muffin wells. Bake at 350 degrees, approximately 30 minutes.

When baked, cool muffins in tins on racks for 10 minutes. Turn muffins out onto racks to finish cooling.

To make yeast muffins, soak a tablespoon or more of yeast in liquid ingredients and then add to dry. Proceed with rest of recipe.

Corn meal muffins can be made by using 1 cup corn meal and 1 cup wheat germ instead of whole wheat pastry flour and other dry ingredients. Honey is better than molasses in this recipe.

Try grinding sunflower seeds to replace some of the dry ingredients for another variation.

Rice polishings or other flour can be substituted for part of the whole wheat flour.

SUNFLOWER SPICE APPLE MUFFINS

Makes 12 large muffins   *Bake at 375*

Really small cakes. Frosted, they can be used for birthday parties.

2 cups w/w pastry flour	2 teaspoons baking powder
1/2 cup wheat germ	□
1 cup sunflower seeds	1/2 cup canola or
2 cups dried apple pieces	safflower oil
1/2 teaspoon salt	1 cup honey or fruit concentrate
1 teaspoon allspice	5 eggs
1 teaspoon cinnamon	2 teaspoons vanilla
1/4 cup powdered dry milk	1/4 cup water

Preheat oven to 375 degrees.

Grease muffin tins.

Mix dry ingredients in a large bowl. Mix wet ingredients in a separate bowl. Combine wet and dry ingredients and mix briefly, enough to moisten batter. Do not overmix or muffins will be tough.

Fill muffin wells 2/3 full and bake for 15-20 minutes, or until muffins are lightly browned and springy to the touch.

Remove tin from oven and let stand 10 minutes before removing muffins to a cooling rack.

These muffins keep for a week in the refrigerator and freeze nicely too.

DATE WALNUT MUFFINS

Makes 12 large muffins   *Bake at 400*

Great served with butter, peanut butter, or cream cheese for a quick weekend lunch.

2/3 cup w/w pastry flour   **1 cup chopped walnuts**
2/3 cup cornmeal   **□**
1/3 cup bran   **2 eggs**
1/3 cup wheat germ   **1/4 cup safflower or soy oil**
1/2 teaspoon salt   **1/4 cup honey**
3 teaspoons baking powder   **1 cup sweet or sour milk**
1 cup date pieces in oat flour

Preheat oven to 400 degrees.

Grease muffin tins.

Mix dry ingredients in a large bowl. Mix wet ingredients in a separate bowl. Combine wet and dry ingredients and mix briefly, just to moisten. Do not overmix or muffins will be tough.

Fill muffin wells 2/3 full and bake for 15-20 minutes, or until muffins are lightly browned and springy to the touch.

Take tin out of oven and cool on rack for 10 minutes before removing muffins.

They may be stored in the freezer and removed in the morning to stick into a lunchbox.

RAISIN BRAN MUFFINS

Makes 12 large muffins   *Bake at 425*

Raisin bran muffins are great to take along on vacations when you need food from home.

1 cup w/w pastry flour   **1 egg**
1 cup wheat bran   **1 cup sweet or sour milk**
1 teaspoon cinnamon   **3 tablespoons safflower oil**
2 teaspoons baking powder   **4 tablespoons honey**
1/2 teaspoon salt   **1 teaspoon vanilla**
1 cup raisins   **1 teaspoon cider vinegar**

Preheat oven to 425 degrees.

Grease a muffin tin.

Mix dry ingredients in a large bowl. Mix wet ingredients in a separate bowl. Combine wet and dry ingredients and mix briefly to moisten. Do not overmix or muffins will be tough.

Fill muffin wells 2/3 full and bake for 15-20 minutes, or until muffins are lightly browned and springy to the touch.

Take tin out of oven and let stand 10 minutes before removing muffins to finish cooling on rack.

Serve muffins slightly warm. Eat within two days, or freeze for later use.

CORNMEAL MUFFINS

Makes about 48 large muffins, freeze some   *Bake at 400*

Make these muffins with white, yellow, or blue cornmeal.

2 cups coarse cornmeal	1 teaspoon salt
1 cup w/w pastry flour	2 cups sweet, sour, or soy milk
or spelt flour	1/2 cup safflower or canola oil
1/4 cup wheat germ	1 cup honey, fruit concentrate
1/4 cup bran	or rice syrup
3/4 cup soy flour	5 eggs
2 tablespoons baking powder	

Using the steel blade of a food processor, blend ingredients with on/off turns just until the batter flows smoothly under the blade, about 10 seconds. Stop machine and scrape down the sides of workbowl with a rubber spatula. Mix again for 2 seconds.

Refrigerate batter for several hours. When ready to use, you will probably have to thin the batter with milk, fruit juice, or water to make it the consistency of heavy cream or pea soup.

Preheat oven to 400 degrees. Grease muffin tins.

Fill wells 2/3 full and bake muffins 15-20 minutes until lightly browned and springy to the touch.

Take tin out of the oven and let stand 10 minutes before removing muffins to cooling rack. Eat muffins within a day or two, or freeze for later use.

CRANBERRY WALNUT MUFFINS

Makes 12 large muffins   *Bake at 375*

These make a wonderful addition to a holiday bread basket.

1-1/2 cups w/w pastry or
  spelt flour
2 teaspoons baking powder
1/2 teaspoon salt
1/2 teaspoon cinnamon
3/4 cup honey or fruit concentrate
1/4 cup safflower or canola oil

2 eggs
1/2 cup sweet, sour or
  soy milk
□
1 cup walnuts
2 cups cranberries

Preheat oven to 375 degrees. Grease a muffin tin.

Blend all the ingredients, except walnuts and cranberries, using the steel blade of a food processor and on/off turns. Stop the machine once or twice to scrape down the sides of the workbowl with a rubber spatula.

Add walnuts and cranberries. Coarsely chop into the batter with several on/off turns.

Fill muffin wells 2/3 full. Bake muffins 30 minutes, or until lightly browned and springy to the touch.

Remove tin from oven and let stand 10 minutes before turning muffins out to finish cooling on a rack. Serve at room temperature, or store air-tight in the freezer. (If serving from the freezer, thaw still air-tight. Then, place muffins on cookie sheet and warm in a 375 degree oven for 5 minutes.)

NEW ORLEANS BLACK MUFFINS

Makes 12 large muffins   *Bake at 350*

Serve these aromatic muffins warm. Best eaten the same day.

2 cups roasted pecans
    □
3/4 cup hot water
1/2 cup molasses
1/4 cup sweet, sour or
    or soy milk

3 cups w/w pastry flour or
    spelt flour
3/4 cup honey
2 teaspoons baking powder
1 teaspoon salt

Roast pecans on a cookie sheet in a 300 degree oven for 10 minutes. Coarsely chop using the steel blade of a food processor. Remove nuts from workbowl and set aside.

Preheat oven to 350 degrees.

Line 12-cup muffin tin with paper liners or grease muffin wells.

Using the steel blade of the food processor again, blend all the ingredients, except for the pecans, until the batter moves freely under the blade.

Add pecans and mix in with three quick on/off turns.

Divide batter among muffin wells. Bake for 25 minutes, or until nicely browned. Remove muffin tin from the oven and let stand for 5-10 minutes. Transfer muffins to rack and cool.

BASIL BISCUITS

Makes 10 biscuits   *Bake at 450*

Serve warm with butter for brunch or dinner.

1 cup w/w pastry flour   □
1-1/2 teaspoons baking powder   2 tablespoons fresh basil
1/4 teaspoon salt   2 scallions, cut into 2" lengths
              □   □
3 tablespoons unsalted butter   1/3 cup milk or soy milk

Preheat oven to 450 degrees.

Using the steel blade of a food processor, sift together the flour, baking powder and salt with several on/off turns. Cut in butter the same way until mixture resembles coarse meal.

Again, using on/off turns, chop in basil and green onions. Add milk and combine quickly with two on/off turns. Remove dough and shape into a ball with your hands.

On a lightly floured surface, roll dough out 1/2 inch thick. Using a 2-inch round cutter, cut dough into 10 biscuits. Arrange on an ungreased baking sheet and bake for 12 to 15 minutes, or until golden on top and dry on the sides.

MOM'S SESAME CORNCRISPS

Makes about 24   *Bake at 400*

Homely, but corncrisps taste great and don't last long!

1 cup boiling water   **2 tablespoons corn or**
     □   **peanut oil**
1 cup coarse cornmeal   **1/2 teaspoon salt**
7/8 cup brown sesame seeds

Preheat oven to 400 degrees.

Bring water to a boil. Combine cornmeal, sesame seeds, oil and salt in a bowl and pour over boiling water. Stir until smooth.

Grease two cookie sheets. Onto cookie sheets, drop corncrisps by tablespoonfuls close together. They don't spread. Flatten crisps using your fingers.

Bake 20 minutes, or until golden brown around the edges. Remove corncrisps with a metal spatula to cool on a wire rack.

Serve with soups, salad, or guacamole. If any crisps remain, store airtight in freezer. Reheat to crisp.

PEPPER ANISEED CRACKERBREAD

Makes 10   *Bake at 450*

Pepper aniseed crackerbread is best eaten the day it is made. Good with soups and salads.

2 cups w/w or spelt flour	1 tablespoon barley malt
1 teaspoon aniseed	syrup
1 teaspoon coarse black pepper	1/2 cup water
1 teaspoon salt	1/4 cup olive or safflower oil

Blend flour, aniseed, pepper and salt using the steel blade of a food processor. While the machine is running, add barley malt, water and oil. Process until a ball forms and cleans the workbowl, about 15-20 seconds. The dough will be smooth. Cover workbowl with plastic or a clean shower cap. Let dough rest 15 minutes. (Can be prepared 1 day ahead and refrigerated.)

Preheat oven to 450 degrees. Grease a baking sheet.

Divide dough into 10 pieces. Work with 2 pieces of dough at a time, making sure remaining pieces are covered to prevent drying out.

Using a rolling pin, roll the 2 pieces into thin 8-inch rounds, like a pizza crust. Arrange on the baking sheet. Bake until light brown, about 8 minutes. Remove crackerbreads to cool on a rack.

Continue the same way with the remainder of the dough.

SOFT CARAWAY BREADSTICKS

Makes 1 dozen long breadsticks   *Bake at 425*

1 tablespoon baking yeast
1/2 cup lukewarm water
1 teaspoon honey
□
1/2 cup safflower or canola oil
1-1/2 tablespoons honey
1 teaspoon salt
1/2 cup boiling water

□
1 egg
□
3-1/2 cups w/w pastry
   flour, approximately
2 tablespoons caraway
   seeds, more at end
1 egg, with 1 teaspoon water

Sprinkle yeast over water and whisk until yeast is dissolved. Add 1 teaspoon honey. Stir again.

Using the plastic or steel blade of a food processor, mix the oil, 1-1/2 tablespoons honey, salt and boiling water. When this cools to lukewarm, add egg and yeast mixture. Whirl again. Add flour, one cup at a time, mixing several seconds after each addition. Add caraway seeds. Blend briefly, with on/off turns of processor, but do not knead.

Refrigerate workbowl until the dough is chilled and firm.

Grease cookie sheet. Divide dough into 12 pieces. On a floured board and in your hands, roll dough into breadsticks about a foot in length. Place 1-2" apart on the baking sheet and brush with beaten egg/water. Lightly press additional caraway seeds into breadsticks. Let rise uncovered about 30 minutes.

While breads rise, preheat oven to 425 degrees. Bake 15 minutes. Remove breadsticks from cookie sheet to cool on rack.

CRISP SESAME BREADSTICKS

Makes 3 dozen   *Bake at 400*

These may be frozen and warmed on a cookie sheet before serving. Caraway seeds may be substituted for sesame seeds.

**3-1/2 cups w/w bread
    flour or spelt flour
1 teaspoon salt
1 tablespoon baking yeast**

**1 tablespoon olive oil
1-1/4 cups warm water
☐
1/2 cup brown sesame seeds**

Using the steel or plastic blade of a food processor, mix 1-1/2 cups of the flour, salt and yeast. With the machine running, pour in olive oil and warm water; process for 30 seconds.

Mix in sesame seeds. Gradually add enough of the remaining flour to make a soft, slightly sticky dough. Remove dough from workbowl and place in a bowl with 1 tablespoon oil. Turn dough to coat. Cover and let rise in a warm place until doubled in bulk, about one hour.

Punch down dough. Divide into 4 hunks and each hunk into 9 additional pieces. Form each piece into a cigar-shaped roll about 6 inches long. Place breadsticks on 3 greased baking sheets, 12 to a sheet, about an inch apart.

Cover baking sheets with a clean towel and let breadsticks rise in a warm place until doubled in bulk, about 30 minutes. While bread rises, preheat oven to 400 degrees.

Bake 20 minutes, or until golden brown. Cool on a rack.

DATE WALNUT TEA CAKE

Makes one large loaf or 2 smaller ones   *Bake at 325*

Yummy with tea. For lunch, spread with nut butter.

1 cup w/w bread flour
1 cup w/w pastry flour
1/4 cup wheat germ
1/4 cup bran
1/2 teaspoon salt
1 teaspoon baking powder
1/4 cup safflower or canola
    oil

3/4 cup honey or fruit juice
    concentrate
2 eggs
2 large, ripe bananas
2 tablespoons hot water
    □
1 cup walnuts
1/2 cup date pieces in oat flour

Preheat oven to 325 degrees. Grease a 9x5 loaf pan, or 2 mini loaf pans.

Blend all the ingredients, except walnuts and date pieces, using the steel blade of a food processor and on/off turns. Stop once or twice and scrape down the sides of the workbowl with a rubber spatula.

Add walnuts and date pieces and coarsely chop into batter with several on/off turns.

Fill prepared pan(s) with batter and bake 60-70 minutes, until bread is firm to touch and a knife inserted in the center comes out clean. When baked, cool in pan on rack for 10 minutes. Turn out and finish cooling on rack. Wrap tea cakes when completely cool. Store a day before slicing.

CINNAMON STICKY BUNS

Makes 18 buns   *Bake at 375*

Sticky to work with, but the end result is worth it!

1 large potato
□
1 tablespoon baking yeast
3 tablespoons honey
1/2 cup warm water
□
1/2 cup soy milk
1/4 cup honey
3 tablespoons canola oil

1 teaspoon salt
4-5 cups whole wheat pastry flour
□
1-1/2 cups maple or date sugar
1 cup raisins or date pieces
1 cup walnuts, chopped
2 teaspoons cinnamon
□
1/2 cup maple syrup

Cook potato in sauce pan and boiling water until easily pierced with a fork, about 30 minutes. Drain and reserve 1 cup cooking liquid. Mash potato and mix in 3/4 cup cooking liquid. Cool to lukewarm.

Sprinkle yeast over warm water and honey in the workbowl of a food processor. Using the steel blade, stir to dissolve with a few on/off turns. Let yeast mixture stand until foamy, about 10 minutes. Add mashed potato mixture together with soy milk, honey, oil and salt. Turn the machine on and off several times to mix. Add flour, one cup at a time, to form soft dough. Knead with on/off turns until smooth and elastic, about 1 minute. Let dough rest in workbowl for 20 minutes. Punch down.

Place 1 tablespoon oil in a bowl. Remove dough from workbowl to oiled bowl and turn to coat. Cover bowl with plastic wrap or shower cap. Let dough rise until doubled in bulk, about 1 hour.

Grease 18 muffin wells. Gently punch dough down. Roll on a lightly floured work surface to form an 18x18-inch square. Mix maple sugar, raisins or dates, walnuts, and cinnamon. Spread mixture over dough, leaving an one-inch border on all sides. Roll dough up jelly-roll fashion to form cylinder. Slice with a sharp knife into 18 pieces.

Place 1 teaspoon maple syrup in each muffin well. Place a sticky bun roll in each well. Brush with vegetable oil. Cover with a damp cloth and let rolls rise again in a warm place until doubled in size, about 35 minutes. While dough rises, preheat oven to 375 degrees.

When risen, bake 25 minutes. Remove tins from oven and set on racks for 10 minutes. Turn sticky buns out of tins and serve warm, bottom side up, so that the maple syrup glaze shows.

CARROT RAISIN TEA BREAD

Makes 2 loaves   *Bake at 325*

Wonderful with a cup of herbal tea. Try it toasted with almond or apple butter.

- 1 cup safflower or canola oil
- 1 cup honey or fruit juice concentrate
- 3 eggs
- 1 tablespoon vanilla extract
- 3 cups grated carrot

- 3 cups w/w pastry flour
- 2 teaspoons cinnamon
- 1/2 teaspoon salt
- 1 teaspoon baking powder
- 1/2 teaspoon baking soda
- □
- 1 cup raisins

Preheat oven to 325 degrees.

Grease two 5x9 loaf pans.

In a large mixing bowl, whisk together oil, honey and eggs. Stir in vanilla and grated carrot.

In a second bowl, mix the dry ingredients. Stir into wet ingredients until moistened. Do not overmix. Fold in raisins.

Spoon batter into loaf pans.

Bake for 1 hour, or until a knife inserted into the center comes out clean. Remove pans from oven to cooling racks. Let stand for 10 minutes. Remove cakes from pans and finish cooling on racks.

Soups

SOUPS

It is almost impossible to make bad soup. A whole meal can be put together by throwing leftover grains, beans, chicken, etc. in a soup kettle. One of our favorite soups is one we will never be able to recreate. We started with leftover barley, roasted chestnuts and asparagus. The resulting soup was yummy, but we can't remember what we did!

Most of the soups included in this section are not only fat-free; they are chock-full of healthful fiber and the nutrient-dense vegetables that should be the backbone of any health-supportive diet. Just add a crusty whole grain bread and a fresh salad and you have a complete meal.

If you are counting your fat calories, be sure to sample Lentil Soup with Brown Rice (p. 85), Red Lentil Soup with Ginger (p. 87), Split Pea Soup (p. 89), Pea Soup with Red Lentils and Barley (p. 90), Mushroom Barley Soup (p. 91), Salsa Bean Soup (p. 93), Instant Asopa (p. 96), Peasant Minestrone Soup (p. 97), Moldavian Vegetable Soup (p. 98), Peasant Potato Soup (p. 99), Gazpacho (p. 115), Russian Borscht (p. 116), and Cold Fruit Soup (p. 118). None of these recipes contains any added fat. Yet they taste rich and delicious.

People ask what base or stock we use for our soups. Lots of chopped onion, minced garlic and herbs!

So get into the soup habit. New combinations are easy and fun to create.

YELLOW SQUASH AND SHRIMP BISQUE

Serves 6

Aromatic and delicious. Serve with crispy, brown bread and a tossed green salad.

1 large onion, chopped
1 green pepper, chopped
1 pound yellow squash, sliced
1 large potato, diced
5 cups water or vegetable stock
    ☐
1/4 teaspoon cayenne pepper

1/2 teaspoon thyme
2 bay leaves
1 teaspoon salt
2 tablespoons olive oil, optional
    ☐
1/2 pound medium raw shrimp,
    peeled and deveined

Place onion, pepper, squash, and potato in a soup kettle with 2 cups water. Steam vegetables until potato can easily be pierced with a knife.

Using a food processor or blender, puree soup and return to kettle. Add remaining water and seasonings. Stir in olive oil, if desired.

Cut each shrimp into halves or thirds, depending on size. A piece of shrimp should easily fit onto a spoon. Add shrimp to soup and simmer 5 minutes. Shrimp will turn pink and flavor soup.

Taste and adjust seasoning. Serve at once.

WILD RICE, CHICKPEA AND ROSEMARY SOUP

Serves 8-10

A soup that surprises by combining the nutty flavor of wild rice with a hint of rosemary.

2 tablespoons olive oil	8 cups water or vegetable stock
5 cloves garlic, minced	3 tablespoons dried parsley
2 cups cooked chickpeas	☐
1 cup soup-grade wild rice	1 teaspoon salt
1 pound carrots, diced	1 teaspoon black pepper
1 teaspoon dried rosemary	

Gently warm olive oil in a large soup kettle. Add garlic and stir until lightly browned.

Add chickpeas, wild rice, carrots, rosemary, water and parsley to kettle. Bring soup to a boil. Cover and simmer for an hour, or until rice is tooth-tender. Season with salt and pepper.

Serve and enjoy!

LENTIL SOUP WITH BROWN RICE

Serves 6-8

Simple and simply superb!

2 cups dried lentils	**1/2 teaspoon celery seed,**
1/2 cup raw brown rice	**optional**
10 cups water or vegetable stock	□
6 cloves garlic, minced	**1/2 teaspoon salt**
4 carrots, diced	**1 teaspoon black pepper**
1 cup tomato juice	**2 cups shredded, dark green**
1 cup diced tomatoes	**leafy vegetables**
2 tablespoons dried parsley	

Place lentils, rice, water, garlic, carrots, tomato juice, tomatoes and herbs in a soup kettle and bring soup to a boil. Lower heat, cover pot, and simmer until lentils are soft and rice is tooth-tender, about an hour.

Season to taste with salt and pepper. Add green leafy vegetables, cover pot and let soup stand 5-10 minutes. Serve immediately and watch it disappear!

LENTIL SOUP WITH RICE AND APRICOTS

Serves 8-10

Apricots in lentil soups are not unusual in the Middle East, Asia or Russia. They lend a sweetness and thickness to soup. Garnish with minced parsley.

2 tablespoons olive oil
1 large onion, chopped
6 cloves garlic, minced
□
1/2 cup raw brown rice
1 green pepper, chopped
1/4 teaspoon cinnamon
1/4 teaspoon cayenne
1 tablespoon paprika
2 tablespoons dried parsley

1 tablespoon chopped fresh
   mint, optional
2 cups dried lentils
10 cups water or vegetable
   stock
1 cup chopped dried apricots
□
1 teaspoon salt
1 teaspoon black pepper

Gently warm olive oil in a soup kettle. Saute onion and garlic until onion is translucent. Add rice and pepper. Stir until rice is coated with oil. Add remaining ingredients (except salt and pepper) and simmer, covered, until lentils and rice are cooked, about 1 hour.

Season to taste with salt and pepper before serving.

RED LENTIL SOUP WITH GINGER

Serves 10

Even if you don't like ginger, you'll love this soup!

4 cups red lentils	12 cups water or stock
1 tablespoon fresh ginger, minced	1/2 cup dried parsley
	☐
1 pound carrots, diced	1 teaspoon salt
3 large onions, chopped	1 teaspoon black pepper
4 stalks celery, sliced	

Place ingredients, except salt and pepper, in a large soup kettle and bring to a boil. Lower heat, cover pot, and simmer for an hour.

Season to taste with salt and pepper before serving.

INDIAN YELLOW SPLIT PEA SOUP

Serves 8-10

In this soup, yellow lentils meld perfectly with cumin, tomato and rice.

2 tablespoons olive oil
2 large onions, chopped
2 teaspoons cumin
□
3 cups yellow split peas
12 cups water or stock
1 teaspoon turmeric

2 cups chopped tomatoes
1/4 cup dried parsley
2 dried chiles, stemmed,
  seeded and crumbled
2 cups cooked Basmati rice
1 teaspoon salt
□
pepper to taste

Gently warm olive oil in a large kettle. Add chopped onion and saute until translucent. Add cumin and stir for one minute until fragrant.

Add split peas, water and turmeric to kettle. Bring soup to a boil, cover pot, and simmer until peas are soft, about an hour.

Add tomato, parsley, chiles, rice, and salt. Simmer for another 15 minutes.

Taste and season with pepper before serving.

SPLIT PEA SOUP

Serves 6-8

A homey soup to share with family and friends.

4 cups green split peas	2 tablespoons dried parsley
12 cups water or vegetable stock	□
8 cloves garlic, minced	1 teaspoon salt
1 pound carrots, diced	1 teaspoon black pepper
a bay leaf	

Wash peas. Place them together with water, garlic, carrots, bay leaf and dried parsley in a soup kettle. Bring to a boil, reduce heat, cover, and simmer until split peas are tender, about 1-1/2 hours.

Season to taste with salt and pepper before serving.

PEA SOUP WITH RED LENTILS AND BARLEY

Serves 12-14

A bowl of steaming soup that's heaven to come home to on a cold day. The longer it stands, the thicker and better it gets. Thin with water or vegetable broth if serving on the second or third day.

1 large onion, diced
5 cloves garlic, minced
3 cups dried mixed yellow and
    green split peas
3/4 cup red lentils
3/4 cup barley
4 carrots, diced

2 stalks celery, diced
1 teaspoon cumin
1 teaspoon marjoram
18 cups water or vegetable
    stock
□
salt and pepper to taste

Add all ingredients except salt and pepper to kettle. Stir and bring to a boil. Lower heat, cover pot, and simmer until peas and barley are tender, about 2-1/2 hours.

Season with salt and pepper to taste before serving.

MUSHROOM BARLEY SOUP

Serves 6

Thick and creamy with barley. Inspired by the earthy aroma of mushrooms.

1 cup barley	**1 tablespoon dried dill seed**
3 cups water	**2 tablespoons dried parsley**
☐	**6 cups water or vegetable stock**
1/2 cup dried mushrooms	**2 bay leaves**
(Formosan is nice)	**1 teaspoon black pepper**
1 large onion, chopped	**☐**
2 cloves garlic, chopped	**salt to taste**
1 pound carrots, diced	**dash cayenne pepper**

In a large kettle, bring 3 cups water to a boil. Add barley. Bring water to a second boil, cover pot and turn heat to low. Allow barley to simmer for 45 minutes.

Add remaining ingredients, except salt and cayenne, to kettle. Simmer soup another hour.

Season with salt and cayenne to taste before serving.

Mushroom barley is even better the second and third days. However, warm gently and add more water as needed. Barley soaks it up!

WINTRY VEGETABLE SOUP

Serves 10-12

The recipe for this thick, mild, wonderful soup was given to us by Barbara Wagner.

1/8 cup olive oil
2 large onions, chopped
5 cloves garlic, minced
☐
2 large potatoes, diced
1 cup dried lima beans
1 pound corn kernels

1/2 pound carrots, diced
2 stalks celery, sliced
3 cups cooked garbanzo beans
4 cups cooked sweet potatoes, pureed
1 teaspoon black pepper
10 cups water or stock
salt to taste

Gently warm olive oil in a soup kettle. Saute onions and garlic until translucent.

Add remaining ingredients and bring soup to a boil. Cover pot, lower heat, and simmer until potatoes and lima beans are tender, about 45 minutes.

Salt to taste before serving.

SALSA BEAN SOUP

Serves 6-8

Thick and hearty, a simple soup to make. Vary the "hotness" by choosing a mild, medium, or hot salsa.

3 cups mixed beans and split peas, or use a soup bean mix	**2 tablespoons dried parsley**
	1 bay leaf
12 cups water or vegetable stock	**☐**
10 cloves garlic, minced	**2 cups salsa**

Rinse and sort beans to check for stones. Place peas and beans in a kettle together with water and garlic. Bring soup to a boil, cover, lower heat and simmer until beans are tender, about 2-1/2 hours. Add parsley and bay leaf and simmer for another 10 minutes.

Add salsa. Taste and adjust seasoning.

HEARTY BEAN SOUP WITH PASTA AND ROMANO

Serves 8-10

Wonderful on a blustery day. Serve as a filling first course, or ladled into big bowls and served with chunks of bread as an entire meal.

2 tablespoons olive oil
2 large onions, chopped
4 cloves garlic, minced
1 red bell pepper, chopped
1 green bell pepper, chopped
4 tablespoons dried parsley
8 cups vegetable stock or water
1 16-ounce can pureed tomatoes
2 cups cooked kidney beans
2 cups cooked navy beans

2 cups small pasta (such as shells or bow ties)
□
2 cups spinach or other green leafy vegetable
1 teaspoon black pepper
salt to taste
□
1 tablespoon Pecorino Romano cheese per person

Gently warm oil in a large kettle and saute onions and garlic until onion is translucent. Add peppers and parsley and saute another few minutes.

Add liquid, tomatoes, and beans to kettle. Bring soup to a boil over medium heat. Cover and simmer 5 minutes.

Add pasta to soup and cook just until tooth-tender and soup is stew-like in consistency, about 15 minutes. Fold in spinach and black pepper, cover, and let stand another 5 minutes.

Taste and season with salt if desired. Ladle into shallow bowls. Sprinkle with grated Romano.

CUBAN BLACK BEAN SOUP

Serves 6-8

Black turtle beans accented with garlic, oregano, cumin, and cayenne pepper.

3 cups dried black beans	**1/2 teaspoon cumin**
□	**1/4 teaspoon cayenne pepper**
1/4 cup olive oil	**12 cups water or stock**
2 large onions, chopped	**1 teaspoon salt**
1/2 medium green pepper, chopped	**1 teaspoon black pepper**
□	□
1 tablespoon dried parsley	**lemon juice, optional**
4 cloves garlic, minced	**jalapeno, minced, optional**
1/2 teaspoon oregano	□
	red onion chopped for garnish

Rinse and sort black beans for small stones. Black beans have more than their share!

Gently warm olive oil in a large kettle. Saute onions and green pepper until soft.

Add parsley, garlic, beans, oregano, spices and water to kettle and bring soup to a boil. Cover pot, lower heat, and simmer until beans are soft and soup begins to thicken, about 1-2 hours. Add salt and pepper.

Using a food processor or blender, blend half the soup. Leave the other half unblended to vary texture. Return blended soup to kettle. Taste and adjust seasoning.

For a tangy version, add lemon juice; for more heat, add minced jalapeno pepper. Garnish with chopped red onion.

INSTANT ASOPA

Serves 8-10

Leftovers? Make soup!

4-1/2 cups leftover vegetables
10 cloves garlic, minced
6-9 cups vegetable broth
2 cups leftover pasta

2 cups leftover grains (kasha,
    barley, rice, millet, quinoa)
salt and pepper to taste

Combine vegetables, garlic, broth, pasta, and grains in a large kettle. Over low-medium flame, heat soup thoroughly. Add salt and pepper to taste.

Remove kettle from stove and cover. Let stand 5-10 minutes to give the flavors a chance to blend. Serve immediately.

PEASANT MINESTRONE SOUP

Serves 12

A meal in itself. Thick and chunky, popular, hard to resist.

10 cloves garlic, chopped
1 red onion, diced
1 cup dried white beans
4 carrots, halved lengthwise and sliced
2 ribs celery, sliced
6 cups water or vegetable stock
   □
2 cups tomato puree
1 cup diced tomato

1/2 cup pitted green olives, halved
1 bay leaf
1 teaspoon oregano
1 teaspoon basil
1/2 teaspoon cayenne pepper
8 ounces noodles or other pasta
   □
1/2 pound spinach or swiss chard, coarsely chopped

Add garlic, onion, beans, carrots, celery and water to kettle. Bring soup to a boil. Cover pot, lower heat, and simmer until beans are tender, about 1-1/2 hours.

Add tomato puree, tomato, olives, bay leaf, oregano, basil and cayenne. Add pasta to soup. Cover and simmer 15 minutes.

Stir in green leafy vegetable. Taste and adjust seasoning before serving with chunks of fresh brown bread.

MOLDAVIAN VEGETABLE SOUP

Serves 6

Light and satisfying. Serve with corn bread and a salad of ripe red tomatoes, olives, and feta cheese.

1 large onion, chopped	2 tablespoons dried parsley
5 cloves garlic, minced	1 teaspoon dried dill weed
2 carrots, halved lengthwise	1 teaspoon thyme
and sliced	1/2 teaspoon marjoram
1 rib celery, sliced	2 bay leaves
1 large green pepper, chopped	dash cayenne pepper
3 large potatoes, diced	1 teaspoon black pepper
2 cups chopped tomatoes	1 teaspoon salt
2 cups fresh or frozen corn	6 cups water or vegetable stock
1/3 cup kasha (buckwheat groats)	

Place all ingredients in a large kettle and bring soup to a boil. Lower heat and simmer, covered, about 30 minutes.

Taste and adjust seasoning before serving.

PEASANT POTATO

Serves 8-10

A simple, old-fashioned potato-onion soup from my mother, Beatrice Stark. The flecks of potato peel make this soup look gourmet!

10 large potatoes, unpeeled, quartered	**10 cups water or stock**
	1 teaspoon salt
5 large onions, quartered	**1 teaspoon black pepper**

Place potatoes and onions in a kettle with barely enough water to cover. Bring to a boil. Cover pot and simmer soup until potatoes are easily pierced with a knife, about 15 minutes.

Take a second kettle and place next to food processor. From the first kettle, remove potatoes and onions in batches to blend. Add liquid from pot as needed so that potato-onion mixture flows under the blade smoothly. As each batch is blended, place in the second kettle.

Add no more water than necessary. Soup should be the consistency of light cream. When soup is blended, stir in salt and pepper. Taste and adjust as needed.

For a richer version of this soup, add a little butter or olive oil.

CAULIFLOWER SOUP WITH BASIL AND PINE NUTS

Serves 8

A fragrant, blended soup. Serve with herb bread slathered with pesto. Ripe tomatoes on the side and fresh peaches for dessert.

2 tablespoons pine nuts	*8 cups water or vegetable stock*
□	□
1 small head cauliflower,	*1 teaspoon dried basil*
broken into florets	*2 tablespoons olive oil*
1 potato, cubed	*salt and pepper to taste*
2 onions, quartered	*1/2 cup watercress leaves,*
	for garnish

Toast pine nuts in the oven at 300 degrees for 10 minutes. Remove from oven and set aside to cool.

Steam cauliflower florets, potato and onions in a large pot with 2 cups water until vegetables are tender, about 20 minutes.

Using a food processor or blender, blend soup. Add liquid as needed so soup flows under the blade smoothly. Return soup to kettle and add remaining water, basil and olive oil.

Season to taste with salt and pepper. Gently reheat.

Ladle into bowls. Garnish with watercress leaves and toasted pine nuts. Serve immediately.

CURRIED SWEET POTATO SOUP

Serves 6-8

A vibrantly-colored soup with a hint of Asia.

2 tablespoons olive oil	**1/4 teaspoon cayenne**
1 large onion, chopped	**1/2 teaspoon turmeric**
2 cloves garlic, minced	**2 teaspoons salt**
1/2 teaspoon cumin	**☐**
1/2 teaspoon coriander	**about 7 sweet potatoes, cut into**
1/2 teaspoon cinnamon	**chunks, assorted sizes fine**
1/2 teaspoon ginger	**5 cups water or vegetable stock**
	lemon juice, optional

Gently warm olive oil in a large kettle and saute onions and garlic until soft. Add remaining spices and stir a minute or two until fragrant.

Add sweet potatoes and water to kettle and simmer until potatoes are easily pierced by a knife. Using a food processor or blender, blend soup until no lumps of potato remain.

Return soup to kettle and warm. Taste and adjust seasoning. Add more cayenne if desired. For tartness, add lemon.

SPICY CURRIED ZUCCHINI SOUP

Serves 6

A fragrant, spicy soup which makes the kitchen smell irresistible.

2 tablespoons olive oil
1 large onion, chopped
2 cloves garlic, chopped
1 apple, chopped
☐
2 teaspoons curry powder
1/2 teaspoon cayenne pepper
☐
2 cups water or vegetable stock

1 cup cooked Basmati or
   brown rice
4 small-medium zucchini
☐
1 quart milk or soy milk
☐
salt and pepper to taste
pumpkin seeds for garnish

Gently warm olive oil in a large kettle. Saute onion, garlic, and apple until soft and fragrant. Sprinkle with curry and cayenne. Stir a few seconds.

Add water and bring soup to a boil. Add cooked rice and zucchini. Simmer 10 minutes until zucchini are easily pierced with a knife.

Using a food processor or blender, puree soup. Return soup to kettle and add milk. Gently heat and simmer 10 minutes, to give the flavors a chance to blend. Do not bring to a boil as milk will curdle.

Season to taste with salt and pepper. Garnish with pumpkin seeds.

Other vegetables can be substituted for zucchini. Potato can be substituted for rice.

CORN CHOWDER

Serves 6-8

Ah, the aroma of olive oil warming in a pot! This chowder is thick and wonderful.

2 tablespoons olive oil	3 cups corn kernels,
1 large onion, chopped	fresh or frozen
2 ribs celery, chopped	1 tablespoon dried parsley
1/2 green pepper, chopped	☐
2 large potatoes, diced	2 cups milk or soy milk
2 cups water or vegetable stock	1 teaspoon black pepper
1/2 teaspoon turmeric	1 teaspoon salt
1 bay leaf	

Gently warm olive oil in a large kettle. Saute onion and celery until soft, but not browned. Add green pepper, potato, water, turmeric and bay leaf. Bring soup to a boil. Cover pot, lower heat, and simmer 15 minutes, or until potatoes are tender when pierced with a knife.

Add corn and parsley and simmer another 3-5 minutes.

Remove bay leaf. Using a food processor or blender, blend half the soup to give it body. Return soup to kettle. Stir in milk. Heat soup, but do not bring to a boil or milk will curdle.

Add salt and pepper to taste, stir, and serve.

SWEET CORN AND CHILE SOUP

Serves 6

A light corn soup from the Southwest with a hint of heat.

1 tablespoon olive oil
2 medium onions, chopped
4 cloves garlic, minced
☐
3 cups corn kernels, fresh or frozen
2-1/2 cups water or vegetable broth
2 hot chile peppers, seeded and minced

2 cups milk or soy milk
2 medium zucchini, quartered lengthwise and sliced
2 tablespoons fresh lemon or lime juice
2 tomatoes, diced
2 tablespoons dried parsley

Gently warm olive oil in a large kettle. Saute onions and garlic. Stir in corn kernels, cover, and cook 4 minutes. Stir in water and chiles. Cover and simmer soup until corn is tender, about 15 minutes.

Using a slotted soup, scoop out 3/4 of corn mixture. Using a food processor or blender, puree. Return puree to soup kettle.

Add milk, zucchini, lemon juice, tomatoes, and parsley. Heat soup, but do not allow to come to a boil.

To serve, ladle into bowls and garnish with more parsley.

ROASTED PECAN SOUP WITH RED BELL PEPPER

Serves 4

Pecans, potatoes, and roasted red bell pepper. A wonderful, rich party soup.

2 tablespoons olive oil	1 tablespoon lemon juice
1 onion, chopped	1 cup roasted, ground
1 clove garlic, minced	pecans or pecan meal
☐	salt and pepper to taste
4 large potatoes, diced	☐
4-1/2 cups water	1 small red bell pepper
☐	2/3 cup milk or soy milk

Gently warm olive oil in a large kettle. Saute onion and garlic until slightly brown. Add potato and 2 cups water. Cover pot and simmer soup for 10-15 minutes, or until potatoes can be pierced easily with a knife. Add more water if needed so potato does not stick to bottom of pot or burn.

Using a food processor or blender, blend soup. Stir in lemon juice, ground pecans, and salt and pepper to taste. Let soup sit covered while proceeding with remaining ingredients.

Roast red pepper under a broiler until the skin is charred. Rinse under cold water and remove stalk, seeds and outer skin. Mash finely and whisk in milk or soy milk.

Heat soup and serve in bowls with red bell pepper mixture spooned on top.

MEDITERRANEAN FISH SOUP WITH WHITE BEANS

Serves 6-8

An easy chowder. As with so many hearty soups, serve with crusty brown bread and a green salad for a complete meal.

1/4 cup olive oil
2 large onions, chopped
2 cloves garlic, minced
2 cups chopped tomatoes
1 bay leaf
1 teaspoon thyme
1/2 teaspoon basil
1 teaspoon grated orange peel
2 tablespoons dried parsley

1/2 teaspoon black pepper
1/2 teaspoon cayenne pepper
6 cups water or fish stock
□
2 cups cooked white beans
1 pound mild white fish (such as haddock) cut into 1-inch pieces
1/2 cup lemon juice
chopped parsley for garnish

Gently warm olive oil in a kettle. Saute onions and garlic until soft. Add tomatoes, bay leaf, thyme, basil, orange peel, parsley, pepper, cayenne pepper and 6 cups water. Bring soup to a boil.

Add the cooked beans, fish and lemon juice to soup. Simmer 10 minutes. Taste and adjust seasoning. Sprinkle with parsley and serve.

Leftover cooked rice or potatoes can be used in place of beans.

SEAFOOD GUMBO

Serves 6

For okra lovers. Serve over brown rice and millet.

2 tablespoons olive oil
2 large onions, chopped
2 cloves garlic, minced
1 green pepper, chopped
1 pint clam juice
1 quart water or stock
2 teaspoons thyme
4 bay leaves
□
1 package frozen okra or
   1 pound fresh, sliced

1 teaspoon black pepper
1-1/2 pounds medium shrimp,
   shelled and deveined (or
   scallops, oysters, crab
   or crablegs)
salt to taste, optional
□
2 cups cooked brown rice
   and millet
1 bunch green scallions, sliced

Gently warm olive oil in a kettle and saute onions, garlic and green pepper until onions are translucent. Add clam juice, water and herbs to pot.   Bring soup to a boil, reduce heat, cover, and simmer 30 minutes.

Add okra, black pepper and seafood to kettle; simmer 10 minutes. Taste and adjust seasoning.

Serve in wide, shallow bowls over steamed brown rice and millet. Garnish with sliced green onions.

[Brown rice and millet are a great combination. To make, bring 2 cups water to a boil. Add 1/2 cup brown rice and 1/2 cup millet, stir, bring to a boil again, reduce heat, cover, and steam for 45 minutes, or until the grains have absorbed the liquid and are light and fluffy.]

INDONESIAN PEANUT BUTTER SOUP

Serves 8-10

Strange combination? No, a winner!

2 tablespoons olive oil
4 cloves garlic, minced
1 tablespoon grated fresh
   ginger root
2 cups diced onions
2 green peppers, diced
□
3 cups water or vegetable stock
3 cups chunky natural, unsalted
   peanut butter

1/2 teaspoon cayenne
□
1 pound spinach or swiss
   chard, coarsely chopped
1 tablespoon fresh lemon juice
4 cups milk or soy milk
salt to taste

Gently warm olive oil in a large kettle. Saute garlic and ginger, stirring until garlic is tender and ginger is fragrant. Add onions and peppers and saute for 5 minutes, until peppers are brightly colored.

Using a food processor or blender, blend peanut butter and water. Whisk mixture into soup, together with cayenne. Simmer 15 minutes.

Remove soup from heat, add spinach, lemon juice and milk. Stir, cover, and let soup stand 10 minutes to give the flavors a chance to blend.

Taste, adjust seasoning and serve.

CHICKEN SOUP WITH HERBS

Serves 4-6

A classic comfort soup. Good for what ails you.

2 carrots, diced	2 cups diced boneless chicken,
6 cloves garlic, minced	either cooked or raw
1 tablespoon dried parsley	1/2 teaspoon oregano
6 cups chicken broth (or	1/2 teaspoon thyme
vegetable stock)	1/2 teaspoon tarragon
1/4 cup raw kasha (buckwheat	1/2 teaspoon black pepper
groats)	1/2 teaspoon cayenne pepper
1/2 cup soup noodles	salt to taste

Place ingredients, except salt, in a large kettle. Bring soup to a boil. Cover and simmer for 20 minutes, or until kasha is cooked and noodles are soft.

Season to taste with salt. Serve immediately.

Chicken broth can be made by cooking the carcass of a chicken with enough water to cover bones for 2-3 hours over low heat. Use turkey bones the same way.

After Thanksgiving, making turkey stock is a great way to get the bones out of the refrigerator. Make stock in large quantities and freeze in glass jars for use during the coming months. Be sure to allow room for expansion when freezing stock.

CHICKEN EGG DROP SOUP

Serves 6

A simple version without the cornstarch.

8-10 cups chicken broth   □
3/4 cup diced cooked chicken   **3 eggs, beaten**
2 tablespoons dried parsley   □
1 teaspoon black pepper   **dash tamari soy sauce**

Bring chicken broth to a boil. Add chicken, dried parsley and pepper.

Slowly pour in beaten eggs, beating constantly with a wire whisk. Eggs will become ribbons.

Taste and adjust seasoning.

POTATO DUMPLINGS

Makes 24 dumplings

Turn vegetable or chicken broth into something special with piping hot potato dumplings!

**2 large potatoes, boiled soft, skin
  left on
1/4 cup hot water, or
  vegetable stock
1/2 teaspoon garlic powder
 1/4 teaspoon oregano
1/4 teaspoon thyme
1/4 teaspoon cayenne pepper**

**1 teaspoon salt
3 tablespoons olive oil or
  chicken fat
3 eggs
1 cup matzo meal or whole
  wheat flour
  ☐
parsley or watercress, for
  garnish**

4 quarts vegetable or chicken broth

Blend all ingredients, except 4 quarts liquid, using the steel blade of a food processor, or mash potatoes with potato masher and mix in remaining ingredients using a wooden spoon.

Chill dumpling batter several hours.

Bring the 4 quarts vegetable or chicken broth to a boil. Drop dumplings by tablespoonfuls into broth. Cover and simmer 20 minutes.

Ladle broth into bowls and give everyone two or three potato dumplings. Garnish with chopped parsley or watercress leaves.

CURRIED AVOCADO SOUP

Serves 6-8

Velvety smooth. Wonderful hot or cold.

1/2 cup finely chopped onion
1 tablespoon olive oil
1 teaspoon curry powder
2 cups water or vegetable broth
2 cups milk or soy milk
4 ripe avocados

1 tablespoon lemon juice
salt and pepper to taste
cayenne pepper to taste
chopped parsley and slivered
    red bell pepper for
    garnish

Gently warm olive oil in a large kettle. Saute onion until soft. Sprinkle with curry powder and add water. Simmer soup five minutes. Add milk.

Peel each avocado and remove the pit. Using a blender or food processor, puree avocados.

Stir avocado puree into soup. Add lemon juice. Heat, but be careful not to bring soup to a boil. Add salt, pepper and cayenne to taste. Serve hot, or refrigerate overnight. To serve, garnish with chopped parsley and a sliver of sweet red bell pepper.

ZUCCHINI POTAGE

Serves 8

Tarragon, thyme, and dill enhance the flavor of this light-textured hot or cold soup.

1 large onion, quartered	*1 teaspoon tarragon*
3 large potatoes, unpeeled and diced	*1/2 teaspoon thyme*
4 large zucchini, chunked	*1 teaspoon black pepper*
	1/4 teaspoon cayenne pepper
5 cups water or stock	*1 quart milk or soy milk*
□	□
1 teaspoon dried dill	*salt to taste*
	fresh dill for garnish, optional

Steam onion, potatoes, and zucchini in a soup kettle with 5 cups water until potatoes can be easily pierced with a knife, about 10 minutes.

Using a food processor or blender, puree soup with just enough water from steaming vegetables so the mixture flows under the blades. Return soup and remaining vegetable stock to kettle. Add dill, tarragon, thyme, peppers and milk.

Stir soup over low heat until hot. Do not bring to a boil or milk will curdle. Turn flame off and let soup stand 10 minutes to give the flavors a chance to blend.

Taste and adjust seasoning. Serve hot or cold and garnish with snips of fresh dill.

SAVORY TOMATO RICE SOUP
WITH HERBED YOGURT

Serves 10

A hint of orange and generous pinches of herbs bring this tomato-rice soup alive! Delicious cold too.

2 tablespoons olive oil	1 cup tomato puree
1/2 teaspoon orange peel	2-3 cups water or vegetable
1 large onion, chopped	broth
4 cloves garlic, chopped	2 cups cooked brown rice
□	salt and pepper to taste
1 tablespoon dried basil	□
1 teaspoon marjoram	Herbed Yogurt, optional
1 teaspoon cumin	1 cup plain no-fat yogurt
pinch cayenne pepper	1 bunch scallions, sliced
□	1 tablespoon dried basil
4 cups diced tomatoes	1/2 teaspoon garlic powder

Gently warm olive oil in a large kettle. Add orange peel, onions and garlic, and saute until onions are soft, about 5 minutes.

Stir in herbs, cumin and cayenne pepper. Cook until cumin is fragrant, about 5 minutes. Add tomatoes, tomato puree, water and cooked rice, and bring soup to boil. Reduce heat to low, cover pot, and simmer 10 minutes.

Taste and adjust seasoning. For herbed yogurt, whisk ingredients together. Place a dollop in each bowl to serve.

GAZPACHO

Serves 12

The flavors of Spain, Portugal, and Mexico in a spicy, cold tomato soup. Best with fresh, ripe tomatoes, but diced, canned ones work fine.

12 large tomatoes, diced	2 jalapeno peppers, seeded
2 pickling cucumbers	pinch each dried parsley, basil,
1 green pepper	thyme, oregano
2 cloves garlic	1/4 cup lemon juice
1 small onion	1 teaspoon salt, optional

Place half the diced tomatoes in a large bowl or soup pot or glass jar. Using a food processor or blender, blend remaining tomatoes, cucumber, green pepper, garlic, onion and jalapeno peppers. Stir blended mixture into diced tomatoes. Stir in herbs and lemon juice.

Taste and adjust seasoning by adding a pinch of black pepper or more lemon. Serve very cold garnished with a sprig of parsley or watercress.

If tomatoes are too liquidy and soup needs body, add a spoonful of tomato puree.

RUSSIAN BORSCHT

Serves 10-12

There are many variations of borscht. This is our interpretation of borscht made for us by Rita Bykovsky. Serve hot or cold.

6 carrots, grated
6 beets, grated
1 large onion, chopped
2 cups diced tomatoes
3 small potatoes, diced
1 sweet green pepper, diced
1 small apple, diced
1/2 head cabbage, shredded
1 cup fresh mushrooms, sliced
1 yellow squash, quartered
   lengthwise and sliced

1/4 cup cider vinegar or
   lemon juice
1 bay leaf
1/4 cup dried parsley leaves
2 teaspoons dried dill weed
4 whole peppercorns
4 tablespoons honey
2 quarts water
☐
salt to taste
yogurt or sour cream, garnish
chopped scallions, for garnish

Using the grating disk of a food processor, grate carrots and beets. Prepare the remaining vegetables and combine all ingredients in a large soup kettle. Simmer 1-1/2 hours.

Taste and adjust seasoning. Serve borscht with a dollop of yogurt or sour cream and a sprinkle of sliced scallions.

Borscht tastes better the second day. So, let it sit overnight in the refrigerator if you can. If you must serve it the day it is made, let borscht sit for several hours to give the flavors a chance to blend.

COLD BEET BORSCHT

Serves 6

Cold borscht, a hot potato in the bowl, and a dollop of yogurt or sour cream make a cooling summer soup. The pink broth is a perfect backdrop for hard boiled eggs and lemon slices.

6 medium beets, grated	6 boiled potatoes
1 large onion, quartered	3 hard-boiled eggs, quartered
1-1/2 quarts water	1 small lemon, thinly sliced
1 tablespoon salt	sour cream or yogurt
2 tablespoons lemon juice	watercress or parsley for
1/4 cup honey	garnish

Using the grating disk of a food processor, grate beets and onion. Place beets and onion in a soup kettle. Add water and salt and bring to a boil. Turn heat off and let pot sit, covered, for 10 minutes.

Stir in lemon juice and honey. (Lemon juice will return color to beets.) Cool soup, then refrigerate until cold, about 3 hours.

To serve, put a hot potato in each soup bowl and ladle borscht over potato. A dollop of sour cream or yogurt gets stirred in. Two egg quarters, a few lemon slices, and a sprinkling of watercress leaves or chopped parsley give the final touch.

COLD FRUIT SOUP

Serves 8

Serve this rosy soup cold. It hits the spot when it's too hot to eat.

1-1/2 quarts water	*1 cup sliced peaches*
1/2 orange, sliced thinly	*1 cup cherries, pitted*
1/2 cup raisins	*2 tablespoons lemon juice*
1/2 cup pineapple dices	*1 teaspoon orange extract*
1/3 cup honey	*1 teaspoon lemon extract*
2 tablespoons arrowroot	*dash cinnamon*
□	*dash ginger*
1 cup blueberries	

Combine water, orange, raisins, pineapple, honey and arrowroot in a large kettle. Simmer soup 20 minutes. Remove kettle from stove and cool soup until barely warm - about 30 minutes.

Add remaining ingredients, mix thoroughly, and refrigerate until very cold.

SOUR CHERRY AND YOGURT SUMMER SOUP

Serves 4

A tart, refreshing cherry soup. Chill thoroughly before serving. Garnish with pitted whole cherries and almond slivers.

2 cups plain low-fat yogurt
1/2 pound pitted fresh cherries
1/4 teaspoon almond extract
1/4 cup fruit sweetener or honey

☐
several pitted whole cherries for garnish
almond slivers, optional

Using a food processor or blender, blend yogurt, cherries, almond extract and sweetener. Flecks of fruit make the soup more attractive, so don't overblend!

Chill 4 hours or overnight before garnishing and serving.

One can substitute peaches, apricots, or even strawberries for cherries.

Salads

SALADS

Our favorite salads are colorful and have a freshness and texture which surprises. We like an unexpected crunch, or a spicy bite in salads. We often ransack the refrigerator looking for something different to throw in.

Have you tried jicama, kohlrabi, grated turnip, or watercress in your salads? Combinations are only limited by the imagination.

Don't compromise on the oil. A fragrant green olive oil, toasted sesame or walnut oil, to name a few, will make a difference.

BASIC TOSSED GREEN SALAD

Serves 4

Every tossed green salad we love has romaine lettuce as its base. The slightly bitter radicchio adds a rich, red color and the turnips add zing.

1 head romaine, washed and torn into bite-sized
pieces, spun-dry in a salad spinner
1 small head radicchio, torn into bite-sized pieces
2 small carrots, grated
1 small turnip, grated

1/4-1/2 cup Debra's Olive Oil Vinaigrette (recipe on page 322)

Place all the vegetables in a large salad bowl and pour dressing over. Toss gently until lettuce is well-coated and carrots and turnips are dispersed.

Serve immediately.

Salad may also be simply dressed with balsamic vinegar, which keeps the calorie count low.

CAESAR SALAD

Serves 4

Garlic, anchovies, and Pecorino Romano. Heaven!

2-3 cloves garlic
1 teaspoon mustard powder
1 tablespoon lemon juice
3 tablespoons olive oil
a 3.5 oz. can anchovies

1/4 cup freshly grated Pecorino
   Romano cheese

☐

1 large head romaine lettuce,
   washed, broken into pieces
   and spun-dry in a salad
   spinner

☐

whole wheat croutons, optional
   (see recipe below)

Crush garlic with a garlic press into a salad bowl. Add mustard, lemon and olive oil. Mash anchovies into dressing with a small fork until almost a paste.

Add romaine to the bowl. Toss until lettuce is well-coated. Sprinkle salad with cheese and toss again. Add croutons if desired. Serve at once.

Croutons:
1/4 cup olive oil
2 cups diced whole wheat bread (1/2" cubes)
2 cloves garlic, mashed

Gently warm olive oil in skillet. Add bread and garlic. Saute over medium heat. Shake pan until croutons are browned.

Alternatively, mix bread with olive oil and garlic and place on cookie sheet in oven. Bake at 350 degrees until croutons are brown and crisp. Stir from time to time.

ENDIVE, WALNUT AND WATERCRESS

Serves 4

Variation on a green theme. Exotic endive, succulent walnuts and spicy watercress. If you can use walnut oil in the dressing, all the better!

Dressing

4 cloves garlic, mashed in a
   garlic press
2 tablespoons lemon juice or
   cider vinegar

3 tablespoons olive oil

Salad

4 heads endive, washed and torn
   into bite-sized pieces
1 head romaine, washed and torn
   into bite-sized pieces

1 large bunch watercress,
   stemmed
salt and black pepper to taste
1 cup walnuts, chopped

Make salad dressing by whisking together garlic, lemon or vinegar, and olive oil.

Wash, spin-dry and prepare greens for salad. Pour dressing over greens and toss lightly with hands to make sure the salad is well coated. Add salt and black pepper as desired. Add chopped walnuts, toss, and serve immediately.

AVOCADO WITH CAULIFLOWER AND ROMAINE

Serves 6-8

Simply delicious! Remember: the fat in avocadoes is GOOD fat!

Salad

2 cups cauliflower florets
□
1 head romaine, washed, torn into bite-sized pieces, and spun-dry in a salad spinner

1 small red onion, halved and cut into thin rings

Dressing

1/4 cup olive oil
1/4 cup cider or wine vinegar
1 teaspoon salt

1/2 teaspoon black pepper
3 cloves garlic, mashed with garlic press

1 avocado

Steam cauliflower florets with 1 cup water until crisp-tender, about 5 minutes. Place in colander and rinse under cold water. Drain and place in salad bowl.

Add romaine and red onion. In a small bowl, whisk together dressing and pour over salad. Toss gently.

Peel and slice avocado. Serve salad using avocado as garnish.

SALAD WITH WATERCRESS, RADICCHIO & PINE NUTS

Serves 6

A tossed, green salad accented with buttery, sweet pine nuts.

Salad

1 cup green beans, cut into
   2-inch pieces
□
1 small red onion, halved and cut
   into thin rings
1 bunch watercress, stemmed

1 head radicchio, torn into
   bite-sized pieces, washed
   and spun dry
1 head romaine, torn into
   bite-sized pieces, washed
   and spun dry
1/2 cup pine nuts

Dressing

3 tablespoons cider or
   wine vinegar
1/4 cup olive oil
1 teaspoon salt
1/2 teaspoon mustard powder
1/2 teaspoon black pepper

4 cloves garlic mashed in
   a garlic press
1 teaspoon oregano
1/2 teaspoon thyme
1/2 teaspoon basil

Steam string beans in several tablespoons of water until crisp-tender, about 3 minutes. Place in colander and rinse with cold water. Drain and place in salad bowl.

Add remaining vegetables and pine nuts to bowl.

Whisk together dressing and pour over salad. Toss gently until romaine and radicchio are well coated. Taste, adjust seasoning, and serve immediately.

SPINACH-LETTUCE SALAD WITH CHOPPED EGG

Serves 4-6

A vibrant, dressed-up version of an old favorite. Dark green, brilliant red, yellow, and white. A colorful taste to match.

1 pound fresh spinach
1 head Boston lettuce
1 small head radicchio
□
1 red onion, quartered and
 thinly sliced
□
2 cloves garlic, mashed with
 garlic press

1/4 cup olive oil
1 tablespoon cider vinegar
 or lemon juice
1/2 teaspoon salt
1 teaspoon black pepper
□
1 hard-boiled egg
nasturtium flowers for garnish,
 optional

Wash spinach, lettuce and radicchio and tear into bite-sized pieces. Spin dry in salad spinner. Place in a salad bowl together with onions.

In a small bowl, whisk together garlic, olive oil, vinegar, salt and pepper and pour over salad. Toss until greens are coated.

Add diced egg to salad. When in season, add nasturtium flowers to add more color and spice. Serve immediately.

SPINACH-CARROT SALAD WITH YOGURT DRESSING

Serves 4

No oil in this dressing. If you don't tell, they won't notice.

Salad
- 1 pound fresh spinach
- 4 carrots, grated
- 1 small white onion, halved and cut into thin rings

Dressing
- 1 cup low or no-fat yogurt
- 1 teaspoon salt
- 2 teaspoons lemon juice
- 3 cloves garlic, mashed with a garlic press
- 1/4 teaspoon oregano
- 1/4 teaspoon marjoram
- 1/2 teaspoon black pepper

1 hard-boiled egg, chopped, optional

Wash spinach, trim stems, and tear into bite-sized pieces. Spin dry in a salad spinner. Place in a salad bowl together with grated carrots and onion rings.

In a small bowl, whisk together dressing and pour over salad. Toss until spinach and carrots are well-coated.

Garnish with chopped egg and serve immediately.

The tartness of this dressing complements the sweetness of carrots. A teaspoon of honey may be added if the salad is too tart for your taste.

NO-OIL DELI SALAD

Serves 6

Cool, crunchy, and multi-colored. Deli Salad tastes like pickles after the first day!

**1 large English cucumber, or
    3 small pickling cukes, cut in
    half lengthwise and sliced
    1/4" thick
2-3 thinly sliced carrots
2 sweet red or yellow bell
    peppers, diced in large
    pieces**

**1 sweet red onion, minced
1 yellow squash, diced
1 kohlrabi, peeled and diced
    □
1/2 cup cider vinegar
1/2 cup water
black pepper to taste**

Combine vegetables in a shallow glass or stainless steel bowl or container. Pour vinegar and water over the vegetables, cover and marinate in the refrigerator for an hour, or longer.

Stir salad every so often if vegetables are not covered by marinade.

Fun to take on picnics. Does not wilt and requires no salt.

CARROT, BELL PEPPER AND RED ONION SALAD

Serves 6-8

Colorful and simple. Serve with broiled fish or chicken and steamed rice.

4 medium carrots, halved and
  sliced thinly in rounds
1 red bell pepper, quartered
  lengthwise and sliced thinly
1 green pepper, quartered
  lengthwise and sliced thinly

1 medium red onion, sliced
  in thin rings
1/4 cup cider vinegar
2 tablespoons olive oil
1 teaspoon black pepper
1/2 teaspoon salt

Place vegetables in a salad bowl. Add remaining ingredients and toss to coat.

Refrigerate, covered, for an hour to give the flavors a chance to blend. Taste, adjust seasoning and serve.

For variety, add steamed, crisp broccoli or cauliflower.

MARINATED MUSHROOM SALAD

Serves 8

A la Grecque. Subtle flavors and contrasting textures.

1 pound mushrooms, thickly sliced	**2 cloves garlic, mashed with a garlic press, or**
1 red bell pepper, quartered lengthwise and sliced thinly	**1/2 teaspoon garlic powder**
4 small zucchini, sliced	**1 teaspoon paprika**
4 whole scallions, sliced	**1/2 teaspoon oregano**
1/4 cup olive oil	**1/2 teaspoon basil**
1/4 cup cider vinegar	**1/2 teaspoon thyme**
	1/2 teaspoon rosemary

Prepare vegetables and place in salad bowl.

In a small bowl, whisk together oil, vinegar, herbs and spices. Pour over vegetables and toss gently.

Refrigerate salad, covered, for several hours. Toss again, taste, and adjust seasoning. Add salt if desired.

Makes a wonderful addition to an antipasto.

TOFU ANTIPASTO SALAD

Serves 12

Cool, refreshing, and a great way to fall in love with tofu. This salad keeps well for 2-3 days.

10 ounces mushrooms, sliced thickly

4 stalks celery, sliced

2 cups fresh or canned tomato chunks

2 sweet green bell peppers, diced

1 bunch Italian flat parsley, chopped

1 package firm or extra-firm tofu, chunked

1/2 cup pitted olives, chopped coarsely

□

2 tablespoons olive oil

1/3 cup lemon juice

1 teaspoon oregano

salt and pepper to taste

Prepare vegetables and olives and place in salad bowl together with tofu. Add remaining ingredients and toss gently to mix. Taste and add salt and pepper if desired.

Marinate antipasto at room temperature for 30 minutes. May be prepared 24 hours ahead and stored overnight in the refrigerator.

THAI TURKEY SALAD

Serves 9

An adaptation of a Thai dish, which is spicy and light. Best eaten the day it's made so the bean sprouts are still crunchy.

2 pounds turkey thigh or breast
☐
4 tablespoons lemon juice
2 tablespoons tamari sauce
3 jalapeno peppers, seeded and minced
4 cloves garlic, minced
1 small red onion, thinly sliced
1 teaspoon dried basil

2 cups mung bean sprouts
2 cups shredded Chinese cabbage
1 small bunch radishes, halved and sliced
☐
black pepper to taste

Poach turkey in simmering water for about an hour, until juices run clear when turkey is pierced with a knife. Remove turkey from liquid and let cool.

Discard skin, remove meat from bones and shred (fingers work fine). There should be about 2 cups turkey meat.

While turkey simmers, stir together lemon juice, tamari, peppers, garlic, red onion and basil. Place in salad bowl, cover and let mixture marinate at room temperature until needed.

Together with remaining ingredients, add turkey to bowl. Toss well. Add pepper to taste.

SMOKED SALMON AND GREEN ONION SALAD

Serves 2

The delicate flavors and pink color of smoked salmon offer a striking contrast to cucumbers and dill. Serve with crisp rye crackers or pumpernickel bread. Finish off the meal with a fruit salad of fresh strawberries and slices of mango and papaya.

8 ounces smoked salmon
1 bunch scallions, sliced
1 long English cucumber, or
several pickling cukes, cut
in half lengthwise, and
thinly sliced
□
several sprigs fresh dill, snipped
into salad

Dressing
2 tablespoons olive oil
2 tablespoons fresh lemon juice
□
1 bunch watercress, stemmed
1 avocado
freshly grated black pepper

Cut smoked salmon into bite-sized pieces and place in a salad serving bowl. Add scallions and cucumbers. Snip in dill.

Mix dressing and pour half over salad. Cover and chill one hour.

When ready to serve, add watercress and pour remaining dressing over salad. Toss gently, taste, and adjust seasoning.

Spoon salad on 1/2 of each plate. Peel, slice avocado and fan slices on second half of plate. Grind black pepper over salad and serve.

TONGOL TUNA SALAD

Serves 6

Tuna salad on the lighter side.

**Three 6.5 ounce cans no-salt
   Tongol Tuna
1 red bell pepper, diced
1 sweet green bell pepper, diced
1/2 medium red onion, diced
2 stalks celery, sliced**

**1/4 cup yogurt
1/4 cup mayonnaise or
   Nayonnaise*
1 tablespoon lemon juice
1 teaspoon black pepper**

Place all ingredients in a salad bowl. Mix with a rubber spatula, but leave tuna in fairly large pieces. Do not mash or make tuna too smooth!

*Nayonnaise is a soy bean mayonnaise which contains no cholesterol. It can be found in any natural food store.

RICE PASTA WITH BOK CHOY AND CASHEWS

Serves 8

Rice pasta combines with bolder flavors and the richness of ground cashews. A salad which keeps well.

10 ounce box Pastariso rice spaghetti, or other rice pasta

Dressing:
4 tablespoon sesame oil
4 tablespoons tamari sauce
1/2 teaspoon fennel seed
1/2 teaspoon dried basil

1/4 teaspoon cayenne pepper
3 cloves garlic, minced
1/2 teaspoon cumin
1 teaspoon black pepper, optional

Salad:
3 stalks celery, sliced diagonally into strips
7 stalks bok choy, julienned
bok choy leaves shredded
1 5-oz. can sliced water chestnuts

1 bunch scallions, sliced
1 cup roasted cashews, coarsely chopped
☐
salt to taste, if desired

Cook spaghetti according to directions on the box. Meanwhile, prepare dressing and place in salad bowl. When pasta is al dente, pour into colander and run under cold water. Shake off as much water as possible and place pasta in bowl with dressing, gently separating and coating strands as you mix.

Add celery and bok choy. Cut scallion bottoms in half lengthwise, then slice. Add to salad together with water chestnuts and cashews. Toss salad until all ingredients are evenly dispersed. Taste, adjust seasoning and serve at room temperature.

CABBAGE SALAD WITH SHRIMP AND WALNUTS

Serves 6

Cabbage is softened by shredding and an acidic dressing. Combined with walnuts, shrimp, and watercress, it becomes elegant!

4 tablespoons wine or cider vinegar
2 teaspoons Dijon-style mustard
1/4 cup olive oil
□
1/2 medium head cabbage, cut into pieces to fit feed tube of a food processor, or sliced thinly by hand

4 whole scallions, sliced
1 bunch watercress, stemmed
□
3/4 cup walnut halves or pieces
1/2 pound small cooked shrimp
1 teaspoon salt
1 teaspoon black pepper
□
romaine leaves for each plate

Combine vinegar, mustard and olive oil in a salad bowl.

Slice cabbage using the thin slicing disk of a food processor and firm pressure, or slice by hand. Remove cabbage to bowl. Add scallions and watercress leaves and toss gently. Chill, covered, for one hour.

Meanwhile, toast walnuts on a cookie sheet in a 350 degree oven for 5 minutes. Remove from oven and cool completely.

Add walnuts, cooked shrimp, salt, and pepper to salad. Toss and serve.

For variety, substitute chicken or turkey for shrimp.

ISRAELI SALAD

Serves 6

Our rendition of salad eaten in Israel for breakfast or dinner. Accompany with thick slices of dark bread and soft white cheese.

6 large, ripe tomatoes cut into bite-size pieces
1 English cucumber, quartered lengthwise and sliced, or 4 pickling cukes, diced
2 red or green bell peppers, diced
1 red or white sweet onion, minced

1 yellow squash, diced
4 tablespoons parsley, minced
4 tablespoons fresh lemon juice
4 tablespoons olive oil
2 cloves garlic, minced or mashed with garlic press
1 teaspoon black pepper
1 teaspoon salt

Prepare and place the vegetables in a salad bowl.

Add the lemon juice, olive oil, garlic, pepper and salt to salad. Mix gently and serve.

CUCUMBER YOGURT SALAD

Serves 4

A simple salad, which is a Middle-Eastern specialty.

1 clove garlic, mashed with garlic press
1 teaspoon dried mint, or 3-4 fresh mint leaves, chopped
1/4 teaspoon salt
□
2 cups low-fat plain yogurt

1 English cucumber, or 4 pickling cukes
□
black pepper and salt to taste
1 tablespoon olive oil
1/4 cup raisins
1/4 cup chopped walnuts

Press garlic into a salad bowl. (If using fresh mint, mash well with garlic and salt before adding yogurt.) Add yogurt, blending completely.

Grate cucumbers with the shredding disk of a food processor. (Alternatively, you can halve cucumbers, then slice thinly.) Fold cucumbers into yogurt mixture together with olive oil, raisins, and walnuts.

Taste and add salt and pepper if desired.

This salad can be made without olive oil, raisins, or walnuts. It will still be refreshing and delicious! It also is wonderful with grated yellow squash and sliced radishes.

Serve at room temperature, or slightly chilled.

GREEK ORZO SALAD WITH FETA AND SHRIMP

Serves 6

Orzo, a rice-shaped pasta, shrimp and salty feta combine the flavors of summer and the Mediterranean. An elegant picnic dish.

Dressing

1/4 cup fresh dill, minced, or
  2 tablespoons dried dill weed
2 cloves garlic, mashed
3 tablespoons olive oil

3 tablespoons lemon juice
3 tablespoons cider vinegar
1/2 teaspoon salt
1 teaspoon black pepper

Salad

1 pound medium shrimp,
  peeled, deveined, and
  steamed until pink
    □
1 pound orzo, cooked, rinsed,
  drained and tossed with
  1 tablespoon olive oil
1/2 cup feta cheese, crumbled
1 large ripe tomato, diced

1/2 cup pitted, Greek-style,
  garlic or jalapeno-stuffed
  olives, sliced
1 bunch flat Italian parsley,
  chopped
1 small bunch scallions, sliced
    □
romaine lettuce leaves and
  sprigs of dill for garnish

Combine dressing ingredients in a large bowl. Add steamed shrimp and toss.

To cook orzo: bring water to a boil in a large pot. Add pasta and cook until tooth-tender, about 7 minutes. Remove pasta to mesh colander and rinse with cold water.

To the bowl, add the cooked orzo, crumbled feta, tomato, olives, parsley, and scallions. Toss gently and adjust seasoning.

Serve salad bedded on a romaine lettuce leaf and garnished with a sprig of fresh dill.

GREEK SHRIMP AND POTATO SALAD
a la PAPPAS

Serves 8

Sunday afternoons, growing up in Florida, we used to drive to Tarpon Springs to order Pappas potato salad. Here's a fond memory of this wholemeal feast.

8 large white potatoes, boiled
☐
8 sprigs fresh parsley, chopped
4 whole scallions, sliced
1 green bell pepper, chopped
1/4 cup olive oil
2 tablespoons wine vinegar
2 cloves garlic, mashed with garlic press
1 teaspoon salt
☐
1 head romaine, washed, torn into bite-sized pieces
☐
12 sprigs watercress
1 unwaxed cucumber, sliced
1 avocado, peeled, pitted and sliced

1/4 pound feta cheese, sliced
4 large shrimp per person, peeled, deveined and steamed 4 minutes
a 3.5-oz can anchovy fillets
12 Greek olives
1 radish per person
1 whole scallion per person
1 ripe tomato per person, cut into wedges
☐
1 tablespoon olive oil per person
1 tablespoon wine vinegar per person
dried oregano

Drain boiled potatoes. When cool enough to handle, peel and slice. While still warm, toss with parsley, scallions, green pepper, olive oil, vinegar, garlic and salt.

Bed 8 dinner plates with romaine. Divide potato salad by mounding spoonfuls in the center of each plate.

Decoratively arrange sprigs of watercress, sliced cucumber, sliced avocado, feta cheese, four jumbo shrimp per person, and anchovy fillets on each plate. Place a radish in the center and a scallion and a wedge of tomato to one side.

Drizzle 1 tablespoon olive oil and 1 tablespoon wine vinegar over each plate. Sprinkle with oregano.

Serve at once. Be mindful that these portions are large. The only thing that should follow this meal is fresh fruit. A bowl of berries would be nice.

POTATO SALAD WITH OLIVE OIL AND OREGANO

Serves 8

Don't stint on the olive oil - it won't be the same! Best served warm. After you taste this, you'll wonder how you ever liked potato salad with mayonnaise.

6 large white potatoes, quartered and steamed in their jackets, or 10 cups little red potatoes, steamed in their jackets

☐

1 large sweet white or red onion, minced

4 stalks celery, sliced
4 hard-boiled eggs, peeled and sliced
1 cup fresh or frozen peas
1 tablespoon dried oregano
1 teaspoon salt
1 teaspoon black pepper
1/2 cup olive oil

When potatoes are cool enough to handle, cut into bite-sized pieces and put in salad bowl.

Add onions, celery, eggs, peas, oregano, salt, pepper and olive oil. Toss gently.

Delicious when served warm.

PEPPERY SLAW

Serves 6-8

Our favorite coleslaw. Entertaining is easy because this is prepared 24-48 hours in advance.

2 pounds green cabbage, cut
   into chunks to fit the feed
   tube of a food processor
8 red radishes, sliced
1 medium sweet red onion,
   sliced thinly
1 kohlrabi, peeled and grated
2 carrots, grated
□

5 sprigs fresh dill or 1
   tablespoon dill seeds
□
1/4 cup olive oil
1/3 cup cider vinegar
1 teaspoon black pepper
1/2 teaspoon white pepper
1/2 teaspoon cayenne pepper
salt, if desired, to taste

Using the slicing disk of a food processor, slice cabbage, radishes and onion with firm pressure. Alternatively, slice thinly by hand. Place vegetables in a salad bowl. Insert grating disk and grate kohlrabi and carrots. Add to salad bowl.

Snip fresh dill into salad using a scissors, or add dill seeds.

Whisk together olive oil, vinegar, black pepper, white pepper, and cayenne pepper. Pour dressing over slaw and toss, mixing thoroughly. Cover and refrigerate. Before serving, stir, taste, and adjust seasonings.

FRESH FRUIT SALAD

Serves 12

Vivid colors, a juxtaposition of sweet and tart, of shapes and textures. A feast for the eyes and tastebuds.

1 quart strawberries, washed, hulled, and halved
2 cups fresh pineapple, peeled and chunked
2 cups washed seedless green grapes
6 peaches or nectarines, halved and sliced into wedges

2 cups blueberries
2 cups pitted bing cherries
4 kiwi, peeled and sliced
1 cup papaya or orange juice
few drops almond extract
□
2 bananas

Prepare fruit as directed above. Use a cherry-pitter, a handy gadget, to plunge pits out of cherries.

Combine fruit, except bananas, with juice and a few drops of almond extract. Toss gently.

Cover and refrigerate for an hour to give the flavors a chance to blend.

Just before serving, slice in banana.

Fruit salad can be as simple as strawberries and grapes combined with a sliced banana or more elaborate than ours with the addition of mango, papaya, etc.

GLOWING SALAD

Serves 6

If you have a food processor, Glowing Salad takes 5 minutes to make. A wonderful cleansing salad, high in iron. Serve bedded on a leaf of romaine and garnish with a sprig of parsley or watercress and a slice of avocado.

2 medium carrots	**1 teaspoon lemon juice**
3 medium apples, halved and cored	**☐**
	parsley or watercress for garnish
3 medium to large beets	
☐	**romaine leaves, for bedding**
2 cups pineapple chunks in juice	**slices of avocado, for garnish**

Grate carrots, apples and beets with shredding disk of food processor. Alternatively, these vegetables can be grated by hand with an old-fashioned grater. Watch the knuckles though!

Place grated carrots, apples and beets in salad bowl and mix with pineapple, pineapple juice, and lemon. Toss until no clumps of apples remain. Add more pineapple juice if salad seems too dry.

Serve as suggested above.

Grain and Bean Salads

BEAN AND GRAIN SALADS

Lunchtime is salad time at The Natural Gourmet. People want a salad that seduces the eye, tastes great and fortifies. Our bean and grain salads hold people over nicely until dinner-time. They also keep and travel well, making them wonderful additions to picnics or potlucks.

RED LENTIL SALAD
WITH RED PEPPERS AND CUCUMBERS

Serves 8

Don't overcook the lentils -- even an extra minute will turn red lentils to brown mush.

1 cup red lentils
2-1/2 cups water
1 red bell pepper, diced
1 bunch parsley, chopped
1/2 English cucumber, quartered
   lengthwise and sliced
   (or use 2 pickling cucumbers)
several sprigs watercress,
   stemmed

4 scallions, sliced (or use 1/2
   sweet red onion, minced)
□
2 tablespoons olive oil
2 tablespoons cider vinegar
pinch cayenne pepper
salt and black pepper to taste

Rinse lentils. Bring water to a boil and add lentils. Cover pot, reduce heat, and simmer 4 minutes. Be careful not to overcook!

Pour lentils into a mesh colander or strainer. Rinse with cold water. Shake gently to remove as much water as possible.

Place lentils in a bowl. Add remaining ingredients and toss gently.

This salad keeps well refrigerated. Bring to room temperature to serve.

DILLED VEGETABLES WITH MILLET

Serves 6-8

Millet, a mild, wonderful grain, is also easy to digest. For a different effect, crumble bleu cheese over the salad.

Salad
- 1 cup millet
- 2 cups water
- ☐
- 2 cups cauliflower florets
- 2 cups broccoli florets
- 2 cups string beans, cut into 2" pieces
- 2 small zucchini, halved and sliced thinly
- 1 small red onion, minced

Dressing
- 1/3 cup olive oil
- 3 tablespoons cider vinegar
- 3 tablespoons lemon juice
- 1 tablespoon fresh dill, or 1 teaspoon dried dill weed
- 1 teaspoon salt
- 1/4 teaspoon basil
- 1/4 teaspoon tarragon
- 1 teaspoon black pepper
- 2 cloves garlic, mashed with garlic press,
- 1 cup bleu cheese, optional

To cook millet, bring water to a boil, stir in grain, cover, and simmer 40 minutes. Turn heat off and leave cover on pot for ten minutes more. Place millet in bowl and fluff with fork occasionally until cool.

Steam cauliflower and broccoli with 1 cup water for about 5 minutes, or until crisp-tender. Place vegetables in a colander, rinse under cold water, and drain. Add to salad bowl. Steam string beans with 1/2 cup water for 3 minutes. Cool under running water, drain, and add to salad together with zucchini and onion.

In a small bowl, whisk dressing. Pour over salad. Toss gently. Crumble in blue cheese if desired. Cover and refrigerate for an hour before serving.

MOROCCAN COUSCOUS

Serves 10

Slightly sweet and very colorful. A favorite with children.

Salad

2 cups couscous
2 cups boiling water
☐
1 cup pine nuts, dry roasted
☐
4 carrots, halved and diced
2 cups green beans, cut into
  2" pieces

2 red bell peppers,
  diced
2 cups peas
1 small red onion, minced
1 bunch Italian flat parsley,
  chopped
1 cup raisins

Dressing

2 tablespoons olive oil
2 tablespoons lemon juice
1 teaspoon salt

1 cup apple juice
pinch cayenne
pinch black pepper

Place couscous in a bowl. Pour over boiling water and let stand 15 minutes for grain to absorb water. Fluff with fork occasionally to cool and break apart clumps of grain.

Toast pine nuts by stirring in a skillet over medium heat until golden, about 3 minutes. Cool.

Steam carrots in 1 cup water for five minutes, until crisp-tender. Steam beans in 1/2 cup water 3 minutes. Place vegetables in colander, rinse under cold water, drain, and add to couscous. Stir in peppers, peas, red onion, parsley and raisins.

In a small bowl, whisk dressing and pour over salad. Add pine nuts and toss. Let stand an hour for the flavors to blend.

RYE BERRY AND BARLEY SALAD

Serves 4-6

Mild, chewy grains combine with colorful vegetables and a zingy dressing. A great summer salad that keeps well.

1/2 cup uncooked rye berries
1/2 cup uncooked barley
3 cups water
☐
1 pound carrots, diced
☐
1 bunch scallions, sliced
1/2 red bell pepper, diced
1/2 green bell pepper, diced
1/2 orange or yellow bell
  pepper, diced

1 bunch parsley, chopped
☐
1 tablespoon olive oil
2 tablespoons cider vinegar
2 tablespoons lemon juice
1-2 teaspoons dried dill weed
1 teaspoon black pepper
1 teaspoon salt
pinch cayenne pepper

Place rye berries and barley in a large pot together with water. Bring to a boil, lower heat, cover, and simmer for about 1-1/4 hours, until water is absorbed and grains are tender.

Place grains in a colander and run cold water over to cool. Shake colander to allow as much water as possible to drain.

While rye and barley are cooking, prepare remaining vegetables. Steam carrots for 3-4 minutes in 2 cups water, or until crisp-tender. Cool under running water. Drain and place in a salad bowl. Add remaining vegetables. When ready, spoon in grains, and pour over dressing and mix well.

As with all grain and bean salads, this is best served at room temperature.

QUINOA WITH PINE NUTS AND APRICOTS

Serves 4

Quinoa, an ancient grain rediscovered, is a complete protein. It also sprouts as it cooks. Because the Indians believed quinoa gave them superhuman powers, Cortez made having it or eating it punishable by death.

2 cups water	**1/2 teaspoon ground coriander**
1 cup quinoa	**2 tablespoons olive oil**
☐	**1/4 cup dried apricots,**
1/2 cup toasted pine nuts	**chopped coarsely**
☐	**1 bunch scallions, thinly sliced**
1 teaspoon salt	**1 red bell pepper finely**
1 tablespoon fresh lemon juice	**diced, or 3 tablespoons**
1 teaspoon paprika	**dried sweet bell peppers**
1 teaspoon ground cumin	

In a medium saucepan, bring water to a boil. Stir in quinoa, cover pot, and simmer for 10 minutes. Turn off flame and let quinoa remain in the covered pot for another 10 minutes so grain will absorb water.

Transfer quinoa to a salad bowl and fluff slightly with a fork every few minutes until grain cools.

Toast pine nuts in a dry skillet over moderate heat, stirring until nuts are golden brown, about 3 minutes. Set aside.

When the quinoa is cool, add remaining ingredients and toss until grain is coated. Serve and enjoy.

RED AND WILD RICE SALAD

Serves 8

Wild rice with its earthy aroma, chewy Wehani or Red Thai rice, and toasted sunflower seeds make an interesting combination. Garnish with marigold flowers in summer.

2 cups Wehani or Thai Red Rice	1 bunch scallions, sliced
1 cup wild rice	1 teaspoon oregano
6 cups water	☐
☐	1/4 cup olive oil
2 cups sunflower seeds	1/4 cup lemon juice
1 bunch flat Italian parsley,	or 1/2 teaspoon salt
chopped	1 teaspoon black pepper
	1/4 teaspoon cayenne pepper

Bring water to a boil. Stir in rice, cover pot, lower heat and simmer 45 minutes. When rice is cooked, let sit in pot with the cover on for another 10 minutes to absorb moisture.

Place rice in a bowl. Fluff with a fork from time to time until cool.

Dry-toast sunflower seeds by stirring in a skillet until seeds begin to brown - be careful not to burn!

Once rice is cool, add remaining ingredients. Mix well. If desired, garnish with marigold flowers, which have a slightly bitter flavor.

Best served warm or at room temperature.

LENTIL BULGUR SALAD WITH FETA CHEESE

Serves 8-10

One of our favorites. Best eaten at room temperature, so it's a great picnic salad, or one to make when you're having company and the refrigerator is full.

1-1/2 cups boiling water	Dressing
1-1/2 cups bulgur	**2/3 cup olive oil**
□	**2/3 cup cider vinegar**
1-1/2 cups lentils	**1 tablespoon dried basil, or**
5 cups water	**3 tablespoons fresh**
□	**2 tablespoons dill seed**
2 bunches whole scallions, sliced	**1 teaspoon salt**
1 large bunch Italian flat parsley,	**1 teaspoon black pepper**
chopped	□
1 green bell pepper, diced	**1-1/2 cups feta cheese**
1 red bell pepper, diced	

Pour boiling water over bulgur and let stand until liquid is absorbed, about 30 minutes. Meanwhile bring 5 cups water to a boil, add washed lentils, and simmer until tender, about 20 minutes. Do not overcook or they turn to mush. Drain lentils and transfer to serving bowl with the bulgur.

Fluff grains and lentils with a fork every once in awhile until cool. Meanwhile, prepare vegetables.

Once grain and lentils are cool, add vegetables. Pour dressing over salad. Toss with a rubber spatula to mix well. Crumble in feta and toss again. Let salad stand, covered, for several hours before serving.

PEA, ARTICHOKE HEART AND CHEDDAR

Serves 12

Pour dressing on warm chickpeas, because they, like potatoes, are more absorbent when warm. This salad is a meal in itself.

Dressing:
- 2 tablespoons olive oil
- 2 tablespoons lemon juice or cider vinegar
- 2 cloves garlic, mashed with a garlic press
- 1 teaspoon salt
- 1 teaspoon black pepper
- 1/2 teaspoon oregano

Salad
- 3 cups cooked, still warm chickpeas
- 2 cups raw or frozen peas
- 3/4 pound cheddar, cubed
- 1 14-ounce can artichoke hearts in water, quartered
- 1 bunch Italian flat parsley, chopped coarsely
- 1 red or yellow pepper, diced

Whisk dressing together.

Place chickpeas, peas, cheddar, artichoke hearts, chopped parsley, and red pepper in a salad bowl. Pour over dressing and toss until chickpeas are coated.

Allow salad to marinate for 30 minutes to an hour at room temperature.

Serve at room temperature.

BLACK BEAN JALAPENO SALAD

Serves 8

Black Bean Jalapeno Salad makes a dramatic presentation and can be tossed together at the last minute if one has cooked or canned black beans.

A colorful addition to a buffet or picnic spread. Black Bean Jalapeno salad travels well and disappears quickly!

4 cups cooked black beans (or 2-16 ounce cans, rinsed and drained)
2 red bell peppers, diced
1 yellow bell pepper, diced
2 green bell peppers, diced
1 bunch scallions, sliced
2 jalapeno peppers, seeded and minced

1/2 teaspoon coriander
2 tablespoons corn oil
2 tablespoons lime juice
1/2 teaspoon salt
1/4 teaspoon black pepper
pinch cayenne

Place black beans in a bowl. (If beans are still hot, place in a colander and run under cold water to cool.)

Add sweet bell peppers, scallions, jalapeno pepper, coriander, oil, lime juice, salt and pepper and toss until beans are well coated.

If a spicier version is desired, leave in a few jalapeno seeds, or add more cayenne.

SOUTHWESTERN SALAD

Serves 8

A vibrant, crunchy salad with the spicy-sweet flavors of the Southwest. Although it can be served cold, we prefer it room temperature.

2 cups cooked kidney, pinto, or navy beans

2 jalapeno peppers, seeded and finely minced

2 red bell peppers, diced

2 green bell peppers, diced

2 cups corn kernels, fresh or frozen

1 tablespoon cumin

2 teaspoons black pepper

pinch cayenne pepper

1/4 cup cider vinegar

2 tablespoons olive oil

1/2 teaspoon salt

□

18 cherry tomatoes, cut in half as garnish

1 bunch scallions, thinly sliced

Combine beans, sweet peppers, jalapeno peppers, corn, cumin, pepper, vinegar, olive oil, and salt. Toss until beans are well coated.

Add tomatoes and scallions, and gently toss salad again. Taste, adjust seasoning, and serve.

ZUCCHINI WHITE BEAN SALAD

Serves 10

Serve as part of an antipasto with roasted peppers, cheese and a loaf of Amy's whole grain French bread, or as a light meal with fresh berries and peaches for dessert.

Salad

- *4 zucchini, thinly sliced*
- *2 carrots, thinly sliced*
- *1 bunch scallions, sliced*
- *1 small red onion, minced*
- *1 cup cooked white beans*
- *1 bunch watercress, stemmed*

Dressing

- *3 tablespoons olive oil*
- *1/4 cup cider vinegar*
- *1/2 teaspoon tarragon*

- *2 cloves garlic, mashed with garlic press, or 1/2 teaspoon garlic powder*
- *1/2 teaspoon dry mustard powder*
- *1/2 teaspoon salt*
- *1 teaspoon black pepper*

  □

- *Greek olives, optional for garnish*

Combine salad ingredients in a bowl. Whisk dressing ingredients together and pour over salad. Toss to mix thoroughly, making sure zucchini slices are separated.

Let salad stand, covered, in the refrigerator for several hours or overnight.

To serve, taste, adjust seasoning, and garnish with olives. Serve at room temperature.

ANTIPASTO CANNELLINI BEAN SALAD

Serves 8

4 cups cooked cannellini (white kidney) beans
2 cloves garlic, mashed in garlic press, or 1/2 teaspoon garlic powder
1/4 teaspoon thyme
1 teaspoon black pepper
8 fresh plum tomatoes, chopped coarsely
2 small red onions, minced
4 small celery ribs with leaves, sliced
1 bunch scallions, sliced

1 teaspoon dried, or 2 tablespoons fresh basil (shredded)
several sprigs flat Italian parsley, chopped
1/4 cup olive oil
1/4 cup wine vinegar or lemon juice
□
salt, if desired, to taste
Extra tomatoes for garnish
Olives for garnish, optional

Place cooked, cooled beans in salad bowl. Add remaining ingredients and toss gently to mix. Taste and adjust seasoning.

Cover salad and let stand at room temperature for an hour to give flavors the chance to blend. (Salad can be prepared a day in advance up to this point and refrigerated, covered.)

Serve at room temperature with wedges of juicy, ripe red tomatoes and olives.

PEPPERY BARLEY SLAW

Serves 8

A variation on coleslaw. Barley, one of the most delicious, digestible and nourishing grains, is jazzed up.

This is another salad that travels well. Delicious the day made, and just as good on the second and third day.

1 cup uncooked barley	Dressing
2-1/2 cups water	**1/3 cup olive oil**
☐	**1/3 cup cider vinegar or**
1/2 small green cabbage, cut	**lemon juice**
into chunks to fit feedtube	**1 teaspoon black pepper,**
of a food processor	**or more to taste**
3 carrots, grated	**1/2 teaspoon white pepper**
1 tablespoon dried dill weed	**pinch cayenne pepper**
1 bunch Italian flat parsley,	**1 teaspoon salt**
chopped coarsely	

Bring water to a boil. Add barley, lower heat, and cover pot. Simmer 45-50 minutes. Place in mesh colander and rinse under cool water. Shake gently to drain.

Using the thin slicing disk of a food processor, slice cabbage using firm pressure. Alternatively, slice the cabbage finely by hand. Remove to salad bowl. Change blade to the shredding disk and grate carrots. Remove to salad bowl. Add dill weed and parsley. Add dressing ingredients and cooked, cooled barley.

Toss gently. Taste and adjust seasonings.

MIDDLE EASTERN TABOULI

Serves 6

In the Middle East, tabouli is wrapped inside lettuce leaves and eaten with the fingers, or served inside pita with tahini sauce.

1-1/4 cups bulgur or cracked wheat	**1 cup cooked garbanzo beans**
1-1/4 cups boiling water	**1/4 cup lemon juice**
□	**1/8 cup olive oil**
1 bunch parsley, minced	**1/2 teaspoon salt**
4 whole scallions, sliced	**1 teaspoon black pepper**
	1 cup diced tomato

Place bulgur in a large bowl and pour over boiling water. Let stand until water is absorbed, about 30 minutes. Then fluff grain with fork from time to time.

When bulgur is cool, add parsley, scallions, cooked garbanzo beans, lemon juice, olive oil, salt, pepper and diced tomato. Toss thoroughly. Let stand, covered, for an hour to give the flavors a chance to blend.

Serve on a bed of romaine lettuce.

Rather than mixing tomato into the tabouli, one can serve slices of tomato on the side as a garnish.

INDONESIAN RICE SALAD

Serves 6-8

A rice salad with an Asian flair. It also travels and keeps well.

Salad

4 cups cooked, cooled, rice (use Basmati, Wehani, or Black Japonica)
1/2 cup raisins
1 bunch scallions, sliced
1/2 cup sesame seeds
1 4 oz. can sliced water chestnuts

1 4 oz. can bamboo shoots
1 sweet green bell pepper, chopped
1 sweet orange bell pepper, chopped
4 stalks celery, sliced
1 bunch parsley, minced

Dressing:

3 tablespoons olive oil
3 tablespoons soy sauce
1 clove garlic, minced or 1/2 tsp garlic powder

1/2 teaspoon ginger
1 teaspoon black pepper
☐
salt, if desired, to taste

Place salad ingredients in a bowl. Whisk together dressing and pour over salad. Toss gently, until rice is well coated.

This salad's mild flavor hits the tastebuds with a delayed reaction.

SPINACH, ZUCCHINI AND FETA

Serves 12

Irresistible and spirited. When zucchini flowers abound in the summer garden, use to garnish.

2 cups uncooked lentils
4 cups water
1 pound raw spinach
2 cups raw or frozen peas
4 medium zucchini, halved
   and thinly sliced
1 bunch scallions, sliced, or 1
   small red onion, minced
   □
1/3 cup olive oil
1/3 cup lemon or cider vinegar

2 garlic cloves, crushed or
   finely chopped
   □
1 cup crumbled feta cheese
1 teaspoon black pepper
salt to taste
   □
zucchini flowers for garnish,
   optional
lemon wedges for garnish,
   optional

Bring water to a boil. Add lentils, cover, lower heat, and cook for 20 minutes, until just tooth-tender. Do not overcook. Pour lentils into mesh colander or strainer. Run under cold water and shake gently to drain as much water as possible.

Coarsely chop spinach. Place spinach, lentils, peas, zucchini and scallions in a salad bowl.

Whisk together oil, lemon or vinegar, and garlic. Pour over ingredients in salad bowl. Crumble feta cheese into bowl with hands, add pepper, and toss salad gently. Taste and add salt if desired. Serve garnished with zucchini flowers or lemon wedges.

RED-LEAF LETTUCE GARBANZO SALAD

Serves 6

An easy and informal dinner salad. Serve with sourdough bread or whole wheat dinner rolls. Honeydew and cantaloupe slices make a grand finale.

Salad

1 cup cooked garbanzo beans □	**1/2 pound spinach, torn into bite-sized pieces, washed, and spun dry**
2 small yellow squash, thinly sliced	**1 cup peas**
1 bunch scallions, sliced	**1/2 pound cheddar or Monterey Jack cheese or soy cheese, cubed**
2 small carrots, grated	
1 head red leaf lettuce, washed, torn into bite-sized pieces and spun dry	

Dressing

1/3 cup olive oil	**pinch each oregano, basil, and marjoram**
1/3 cup cider vinegar	**1/2 teaspoon salt**
4 cloves garlic mashed in a garlic press	**1 teaspoon black pepper**

Place warm garbanzo beans in a salad bowl.

In a small bowl, whisk dressing together and pour over beans.

Prepare vegetables as directed above and add, together with cheese, to salad. Toss gently until lettuce and spinach leaves are well coated and cheese is evenly distributed.

Serve immediately.

FAGIOLIO (HARICOT BEANS) WITH CHICKEN

Serves 4

Fagiolio with chicken makes a light meal with crusty brown bread warm from the oven, or is a wonderful addition to a colorful antipasto.

Salad
- **2 cups cooked haricot beans**
- **1 cup cooked, boned chicken, shredded**
- **1 bunch watercress, stemmed**
- **1 medium white onion, minced**
  - ☐
- **1/2 medium head cabbage, finely shredded**

Dressing
- **4 tablespoons olive oil**
- **4 tablespoons lemon juice**
- **1 tablespoon dried basil**
- **1/2 teaspoon salt**
- **1 teaspoon black pepper**
  - ☐
- **black olives for garnish, optional**

Place haricot beans, chicken, watercress leaves and minced onion into a serving bowl.

Cut cabbage in chunks to fit feed tube of a food processor and finely shred using the slicing disk. Add cabbage to salad. Alternatively, slice finely by hand.

Whisk together dressing ingredients. Pour over salad and toss until mixed. Taste and adjust seasoning. Serve garnished with black olives.

APPLE PEANUT CURRY SALAD

Serves 8

Contrasting tastes and textures. Serve on a bed of red and green leaf lettuce.

Dressing:
- **1 quart plain low or no-fat yogurt**
- **1 teaspoon curry powder**
- **2 tablespoons lemon juice**
- **pinch cayenne pepper**

Salad
- **6 large tart apples (Granny Smiths are great), wedged with apple slicer**
- **1 cup cooked chickpeas, drained**
- **1 small red onion, diced, optional**
- **1 cup roasted peanuts**
- **1 cup date pieces in oat flour**

Make dressing and place in salad bowl. Cut apples into wedges. If apples are large and a wedge won't fit comfortably into the mouth, cut again in half. Place apples in bowl and coat with dressing to prevent browning. Add remaining ingredients. Mix, chill for an hour and serve.

Best served the day it's made so the apples are nice and crisp. Curry intensifies and yogurt thickens as the salad stands.

Pasta and Cheese
Main Dishes

PASTA AND CHEESE MAIN DISHES

If I had to choose one food to take to a desert island, it would be pasta. Pasta is such a wonderful comfort food. Choose your favorite shape, size or color for the recipes which follow. Choose pasta made from Jerusalem artichoke flour, whole wheat, rice or spelt flours. Choose pastas flavored with garlic and parsley, tomato and basil, etc. The list is endless.

Contrary to custom, a pound of pasta in the Stark family feeds two. And this after a large green salad! We have compromised and used a pound of pasta for 4 people. I simply can't believe other cookbooks which feed 5 or 6 people on a pound of pasta!

As for our cheese dishes, we guarantee they taste delicious, but many of then are too high in fat for everyday consumption, and should be passed over by those who are watching their fat intake for health reasons. When you do decide to indulge in Cheesy Vegetable Lasagna or Spaghetti with Olive Oil and Garlic, skip dessert and keep your fat intake low for the rest of your meals that day. Often, the amounts of cheese or oil in these recipes can be cut in half with no loss of flavor. Experiment!

POLENTA PIE

Serves 8   *Bake at 350*

Polenta
> 1 cup cornmeal
> 1/2 cup corn grits
> 3 cups water

> 2 tablespoons olive oil
> 1 teaspoon black pepper
> 1/4 cup grated Pecorino
>   cheese

Filling
> 1/4 cup olive oil
> 4 cloves garlic
> 4 cups chopped onions
> 2 medium carrots, diced
> 4 celery stalks, diced
> 3 tablespoons dried basil
> 2 teaspoons dried oregano
> 1 teaspoon black pepper

> □
> 2 red bell peppers, diced
> 2 medium zucchini, diced
> 1 cup pureed tomatoes
> □
> 2 cups grated melting cheese
>   of choice, (12 ounces)
>   cheddar, pepperjack, etc.

Bring water to a boil. Add cornmeal and corn grits, stirring with a wire whisk until no lumps remain. Add olive oil, pepper, and allow polenta to simmer 10 minutes. Stir often to prevent sticking. Remove from heat and spoon into greased 12x17 baking pan. Cool polenta while preparing filling.

In a large skillet, gently warm olive oil. Saute garlic and onions until tender. Add carrots, celery, herbs and spices. Simmer 5 minutes. Carrots will begin to soften. Add peppers, zucchini, and tomato puree and simmer another 5 minutes. Spoon vegetables onto polenta. Top with grated cheese and bake uncovered at 350 degrees for 30 minutes.

Allow casserole to rest 15 minutes before cutting to serve.

SPINACH FRITADA

Serves 12-16   *Bake at 350*

A snap to prepare, spinach fritada is delicious hot, warm, or cold.

3 pounds spinach, chopped
   ☐
4 slices whole wheat bread
4 cups grated cheddar,
  pepperjack, mozzarella, or
  other cheese
12 eggs

2 pounds ricotta, cottage
  or farmers'cheese
1/2 cup Pecorino Romano
  cheese
1 teaspoon black pepper
1/2 teaspoon nutmeg

Preheat oven to 350 degrees.   Grease a 12x17 baking dish.

Place chopped spinach in a large mixing bowl.

Using the steel blade of a food processor, blend bread into crumbs. Add eggs, ricotta, 2 cups grated cheese, pepper and nutmeg. Add cheese and egg mixture to chopped spinach and mix well.   Spoon mixture into baking pan.   Cover with remaining grated cheese and bake 45 minutes, or until top is golden and firm to the touch.

Remove fritada from oven and let sit for 15 minutes before cutting to serve.

TAMALE PIE

Serves 8   *Bake at 350*

A crunchy crust with spiced beans and a melted cheese topping.

Filling:

1 tablespoon olive oil	**1 tablespoon chili powder**
1 onion, chopped	**1-1/2 teaspoons salt**
2 cloves garlic, minced	**1/4 cup sliced olives**
4 cups diced tomatoes	**4 cups cooked beans (kidney,**
1 green pepper, chopped	**lima, or black turtle are nice)**
1 cup tomato puree	

Crust:

3 cups water	**1 tablespoon olive oil**
1/2 cup corn grits	**1 tablespoon Pecorino**
1/2 cup cornmeal	**Romano cheese**

**2 cups grated cheese or soy cheese of your choice
(one that melts well)**

For the filling, gently warm olive oil in a skillet. Saute onions and garlic until soft, about 5 minutes. Add tomatoes, pepper, tomato puree, chili powder, salt and olives and simmer mixture 10 minutes. Add beans and simmer another 10.

For the crust, bring the water to a boil. Stir in corn grits and cornmeal. Whisk until no lumps remain. Add olive oil and Romano. Simmer 10 minutes. Stir often to prevent sticking.

Grease a 2-quart casserole and spoon in cornmeal crust, reserving 1-1/2 cups for topping. Spread filling over crust and remaining cornmeal over the top. Place grated cheese over all. Bake 30 minutes at 350. Let stand 10 minutes before serving.

CHEESE NOODLE KUGEL

Serves 6-8   *Bake at 350*

Noodles with the tang of cottage cheese and ginger.

1 pound cottage cheese   **drop lemon extract**
2 egg yolks   **1/2 cup raisins**
1/2 teaspoon salt   □
2 tablespoons honey   **1 pound egg noodles**
1/8 teaspoon ginger

Mix cottage cheese, egg yolks, salt, honey, ginger, lemon and raisins together.

Bring water to a boil in a large pot. Add pasta and cook until al dente, firm to the tooth, about 7 minutes. Pour pasta into a colander and rinse with cold water.

Preheat oven to 350 degrees.

Toss pasta and cheese mixture until well blended.

Place kugel in a greased casserole and bake 20 minutes, or until piping hot.

GRANDMA SARAH'S FARMER CHEESE BLINTZES

Makes 14-16

Made without flour. Grandma Sarah used bitter almonds from apricot pits to flavor her filling. Serve for breakfast or lunch drizzled with honey and accompanied by fresh berries.

Crepes

6 eggs
1/4 cup water or milk

2 tablespoons butter
for frying

Beat eggs and water with a fork until foamy. Heat a 10-inch frying pan over medium heat. Add 1/4 teaspoon butter. Turn down flame before pouring in a scant 1/4 cup egg batter. Quickly tilt pan to spread crepe. Patch holes, if any, in blintz with a drop of batter. When blintz underside is lightly browned, turn onto a plate. Do not try to unfold or straighten while hot.

Dot butter in pan and start second blintz. Continue buttering, swirling batter, and dumping crepes onto plate until batter is used. When crepes are cool, straighten and unfold onto a clean plate. Cover with plastic wrap to prevent drying out until filled.

Filling

**1 pound farmer cheese (available
    at delicatessen counters)**
6 tablespoons honey

dash cinnamon
1/2 teaspoon vanilla
4 almonds

Blend filling until almonds are finely ground.

Final Preparation

Place heaping tablespoon of filling on end of blintz nearest you. Fold sides in and roll blintz away, as for egg rolls or stuffed grape leaves. When finished, refrigerate blintzes, covered.

PIZZA CRUST

Makes 3 12-inch pizzas   *Bake at 350, 400*

Herbs and garlic give the crust a wonderful flavor.

2 cups whole wheat pastry flour
2 cups whole wheat bread flour   **4 cloves garlic**
1 teaspoon salt   **1/2 cup olive oil**
❑   ❑
2 tablespoons baking yeast   **1/2 teaspoon each oregano,**
1-1/2 cups lukewarm water   **thyme, basil, marjoram**
2 teaspoons honey

Whirl flour and salt together using the steel blade of a food processor. Sprinkle yeast over lukewarm water and stir to dissolve. Add honey. Pour into workbowl and process by turning motor on/off, 8 times. Add garlic and olive oil. Whirl until dough forms a ball, 15-20 seconds. Add water, a teaspoon at a time, if dough will not form a ball, or a bit more flour if dough is sticky. Add herbs and knead another minute.

Divide dough into three equal pieces. Shape each into a ball and cover. Let rise in a warm, draft-free location for two hours, or until doubled in bulk.

Preheat oven to 350 degrees. Roll each ball out on a greased pizza pan. Press dough out toward edges of the pan with the heel of your hands until dough covers pans thinly. Brush crusts with olive oil and bake 15 minutes.

Remove from oven and top with a favorite sauce, cheeses, and imagination! Turn oven to 400 degrees. Bake pizzas 15 minutes. Let stand 10 minutes before serving to cries of delight.

PIZZA TOPPINGS

anchovy fillets
sliced mushrooms
chopped or sliced onions
chopped or slivered green pepper
fresh garlic, minced
oil-cured black olives
hot chiles
thinly minced Fakin' Bacon or tempeh
pesto

PIZZA SAUCE

4 cups tomato puree
4 tablespoons olive oil
1/4 teaspoon thyme
1/4 teaspoon black pepper
1/4 teaspoon cayenne pepper

1/4 teaspoon oregano
1/4 teaspoon marjoram
1/4 teaspoon basil
1/2 teaspoon garlic powder

Stir pizza sauce ingredients together and simmer over low heat for 15 minutes.

ASSEMBLING PIZZAS

Brush pizza crust with olive oil and cover with sauce (amount to taste). Spread over pizzas a combination of 2 cups grated cheeses -- mozzarella and scamorze, thinly sliced gorgonzola, provolone, fontina, pepperjack, or goat cheeses. Sprinkle with freshly grated Romano cheese. Decorate with favorite combination of pizza toppings.

Alternatively, omit tomato sauce and go right onto toppings. Use lots of fresh garlic.

RATATOUILLE FRENCH BREAD PIZZAS

Makes 6 pizzas   *Bake at 350*

Whole wheat French bread topped with ratatouille and spicy
pepperjack cheese. Soy cheese works fine too.

1/4 cup olive oil	1/2 teaspoon black pepper
1 large onion, chopped	pinch cayenne pepper
4 cloves garlic, minced	1 teaspoon dried basil
1 medium eggplant, unpeeled,	1/2 teaspoon oregano
cut into 1/2-inch cubes	1/2 teaspoon thyme
2 small zucchini, diced	☐
1 red bell pepper, chopped	1 whole wheat French bread,
☐	sliced in half lengthwise,
1/4 cup pitted olives, chopped	then crosswise into three
2 cups tomatoes, chopped	

4 cups, about 16 ounces, grated cheese of choice: perhaps provolone,
mozzarella, and pepperjack cheeses

Gently warm olive oil in a skillet. Saute onion and garlic
until softened, about 5 minutes. Add eggplant, zucchini, and bell
pepper. Saute 5 minutes. Cover and simmer until vegetables are
tender, 10 minutes.   Add olives, tomatoes, pepper and herbs.
Simmer, uncovered, until most of liquid evaporates and mixture
thickens, about 15 minutes.

Arrange bread on baking sheet. Spread 1 cup grated cheese
over bread. Top with ratatouille and then with remaining cheese.

Bake pizzas until cheese is bubbly. Serve piping hot.

CHEESY VEGETABLE LASAGNA

Serves 8   *Bake at 350*

Highly caloric, but when you've gotta, you've gotta.

1 pound spinach lasagna
   noodles
1 tablespoon olive oil
   ☐
1-1/2 pounds pepperjack cheese
1/2 pound provolone
1 pound mozzarella
   ☐
2 pounds ricotta cheese
1 cup grated Pecorino Romano
1/2 teaspoon black pepper
1/2 teaspoon each oregano and thyme
1 teaspoon garlic powder

☐
2 cups tomato sauce
☐
1 pound vegetables of your
   choice, such as broccoli
   florets, cauliflower florets,
   chopped spinach or sliced
   mushrooms
   or
4 cups ratatouille instead
   of vegetables and tomato
   sauce

Cook lasagna noodles in boiling water for 5 minutes. Rinse in colander under cold water and drain. Put back into pot and add olive oil. Stir to coat to prevent sticking.

Using the shredding disk of a food processor, grate cheeses.

In a large bowl, mix together ricotta, Romano, herbs, garlic and half the cheeses you just grated.

In a 13x9-inch deep baking pan, layer half the lasagna noodles. Cover with ricotta mixture. Spoon vegetables or ratatouille over mixture. Cover with second layer of noodles. Spoon tomato sauce over pasta (skip this if using ratatouille) and spread grated cheese on top. Cover with foil and bake lasagna 45 minutes. Let stand 10 minutes before cutting.

MARY'S NOT-SO-HEAVY LASAGNA

Serves 8   *Bake at 350*

Luscious fare on the lighter side!

3 tablespoons olive oil
1 large onion, diced
1 green bell pepper, diced
3 cloves garlic, minced
1 rib celery, diced
1 carrot, diced
1 pound mushrooms, sliced
□
2 8-ounce cans tomato puree
16 ounce can whole tomatoes
 with juice
1 tablespoon basil
1 tablespoon oregano
1 teaspoon salt
1/4 teaspoon crushed red pepper
2 bay leaves
2 tablespoons lite tamari

1/4 cup red wine, optional
□
12 lasagna noodles
□
1 pound tofu
1 pound non-fat cottage
 cheese
2 egg whites
1/4 cup Pecorino Romano
 cheese
1 pound raw spinach, chopped
1 teaspoon black pepper
□
3 cups sliced zucchini
□
8 ounces part-skim mozzarella,
 grated

Gently warm olive oil in skillet. Saute onion, pepper, garlic, celery, carrot and mushrooms. Add tomato puree, tomatoes, herbs and seasonings. Simmer 1 hour. If you can, refrigerate sauce overnight to give the flavors a chance to blend.

Cook the lasagna noodles in boiling water for 5 minutes. Rinse in colander under cold water and drain.

In a food processor, puree tofu, cottage cheese and egg whites. Stir in Romano, spinach and pepper.

To assemble, cover the bottom of a 13x9-inch pan with some sauce. Alternate layers using noodles, cheese and tofu mixture, sliced zucchini, and then more sauce. Repeat twice and end with sauce. Top lasagna with mozzarella cheese.

Bake in a 350 degree oven for 1 hour. Let lasagna sit in pan 10 minutes before cutting to rave reviews.

DALE LAURIAN'S VEGETABLE PIE

Serves 6   *Bake at 350*

A salad and crusty rolls added to this dish make a great light buffet or Sunday supper for the family. Make part of the recipe ahead to cut down on last minute work.

1 eggplant (1 or 1-1/4 pounds)	3 tablespoons fresh
□	parsley, chopped
1 medium Spanish onion	fresh ground black pepper,
2-3 cloves garlic, crushed	to taste
2 tablespoons olive oil	□
□	6 eggs
3 young summer squash	□
1/2 large red bell pepper	12 ounces part-skim
□	mozzarella, shredded
1/2 teaspoon dried basil	1/2 cup grated Pecorino
1/2 teaspoon dried oregano	Romano

Slice eggplant in 3/4" slices. Arrange on a double layer of paper towels. Salt both sides and cover with a second double layer paper towels. Use cutting board or marble pastry sheet to weight eggplant. Drain for 1/2 hour.

Meanwhile, cut onion in half and slice in 1/8" slices. Add 2 tablespoons olive oil to a fry pan or electric skillet. Over medium-low heat, saute onion until translucent, about 10 minutes. During the last two minutes, add crushed garlic and mix well. Remove garlic/onion mixture to large bowl.

Slice squash in thin pieces. Remove large woody seeds if using mature vegetable. Slice red pepper. Add to fry pan with just enough water to steam vegetable until crunchy, crisp stage. Add to onion/garlic mixture.

Rinse eggplant to remove salt. Cut into cubes and add to fry pan with just enough water to steam. Do not overcook, eggplant should be soft but hold its shape.

Peel and seed tomatoes. (Tomatoes peel easily if dipped into boiling water for 30-60 seconds and then plunged into cold water.) Remove seeds with fingers over strainer to save juice. Chop tomato and cook in saucepan with strained juice. Add pepper, basil, oregano and parsley and cook until tomato is soft and juice is mostly condensed.

Add tomato and eggplant to large bowl. The recipe may be prepared to this point three days prior to use. Bring vegetable mixture to room temperature before proceeding.

Beat eggs well with wire whisk or electric beater. Add 1/4 cup grated Romano. Add to vegetable mixture. Spoon 1/2 mixture into deep 10" pie plate. Sprinkle with 1/2 mozzarella. Spoon remaining vegetable mixture into dish. Sprinkle remaining mozzarella and Romano on top. Bake in 350 oven for 40 minutes, or until cheese is lightly brown.

SPAGHETTI WITH WHITE CLAM SAUCE

Serves 4

Clams infused with garlic and olive oil atop spaghetti.

1/2 cup grated Pecorino Romano cheese
1/2 cup olive oil
1 large onion, chopped
4 cloves garlic, minced
□
8 ounces chopped clams

several sprigs parsley, chopped
1/4 teaspoon cayenne pepper
1/2 teaspoon black pepper
1-1/2 cups bottled clam juice
□
1 pound spaghetti

In a skillet, gently warm olive oil over medium heat. Saute onion and garlic, stirring as needed, until the onion is transparent, about 5 minutes. Add clams, liquid and all, parsley, red and black pepper, and clam juice to skillet. Bring sauce to a boil. Reduce heat and simmer, uncovered, 15 minutes.

While the sauce is simmering, bring 4 quarts water to a rollicking boil and cook pasta until al dente, firm to the tooth. Test after 7 minutes by biting. Drain and place pasta in a large bowl or on individual plates. Pour sauce over pasta and serve immediately. Pass the grated cheese!

SPAGHETTI WITH OLIVE OIL AND GARLIC

Serves 4

The simplest and most delicious way of all to eat pasta.

1 cup grated Pecorino Romano   **1/2 teaspoon black pepper**
1/2 cup olive oil   **1/4 teaspoon red pepper**
4 cloves garlic   **☐**
1/2 teaspoon dried basil   **1 pound spaghetti**
1/2 teaspoon oregano

In a skillet, gently warm olive oil over low heat. Crush garlic with a garlic press and add to oil. Warm until garlic is golden, but be careful not to burn. Add basil, oregano, and pepper. Turn off heat.

Bring 4 quarts water to a rollicking boil. Add spaghetti and stir gently. When pasta is al dente, firm to the tooth, about 7 minutes, drain and place in a large bowl or onto individual plates. Pour oil with garlic and herbs over pasta. Mix gently.

Serve immediately and pass grated cheese.

ANCHOVY PUTTANESCA WITH PASTA

Serves 6

A mildly spicy sauce which tastes wonderful hot or cold.

grated Pecorino Romano, optional
□
2 tablespoons olive oil
3 cloves garlic
□
3.5-ounce can anchovy fillets
□
4 cups tomato puree

2 sprigs fresh basil, minced
1/2 teaspoon marjoram
1 teaspoon oregano
3 teaspoons dried hot pepper flakes
black pepper, to taste
□
1-1/2 pounds spaghetti

Gently warm olive oil in a skillet. Crush garlic with a garlic press and saute in oil until golden. Add anchovy fillets and mash with a fork. Add tomato puree, basil, marjoram, oregano and pepper to skillet. Simmer sauce 15 minutes, stirring occasionally, until quite flavorful and thickened.

While sauce is simmering, bring 4 quarts water to a rollicking boil. Add spaghetti and stir gently. When pasta is al dente, firm to the tooth, about 7 minutes, drain and place in a large bowl. Spoon sauce over pasta and mix gently until well coated.

Serve immediately and pass the grated cheese.

SPAGHETTI WITH ARTICHOKE HEARTS

Serves 4-6

A lovely pasta dish. Accompany with a tossed green salad and sliced peaches for dessert.

1/2 cup grated Pecorino Romano cheese	□
	1 teaspoon salt
1/2 cup olive oil	**1/2 teaspoon pepper**
2 small onions, minced	**1/4 teaspoon oregano**
2 cloves garlic, pressed	**1 can (28 ounces) plum**
1/2 pound mushrooms, thickly sliced	**tomatoes**
8 ounces artichoke hearts (water packed or frozen)	□
	1-1/2 pounds spaghetti

In a skillet, gently warm olive oil. Add onions, garlic, mushrooms and artichoke hearts. Simmer, stirring as needed, 10 minutes. Sprinkle with seasonings. Add tomatoes with liquid, mashing as you add them. Bring sauce to a boil, lower heat and simmer 1 hour uncovered.

When sauce is almost done, bring 4 quarts water to a boil, add pasta and cook until al dente, about 7 minutes.

Drain pasta and place in a large bowl. Spoon over half the sauce and toss gently.

Serve immediately with remaining sauce ladled on top. Pass the grated cheese.

MARUZZINE WITH CAULIFLOWER AND CHEESES

Serves 6-8   *Bake at 350*

Cauliflower, pasta, and melted cheeses create a smooth, rich dish.
Serve with sliced tomatoes and cucumbers.

1/2 cup grated Pecorino Romano
□
**2 pounds maruzzine (shell-shaped
pasta) cooked and drained**
□
1 pound part-skim mozzarella
1 pound provolone
□
1 pound mushrooms, sliced
1 head cauliflower florets

4 tablespoons olive oil
1/2 teaspoon black pepper
1 teaspoon garlic powder
1/2 teaspoon oregano
1/2 teaspoon basil
1/2 teaspoon marjoram
1 cup tomato sauce
□
parsley sprigs for garnish

Preheat oven to 350 degrees.

Bring 4 quarts water to a rollicking boil and stir in pasta.
Cook until al dente, about 7 minutes. In a colander, rinse pasta
with cold water and drain. Set aside.

Grate mozzarella and provolone using the shredding disk of
a food processor and medium pressure.

In a casserole, combine pasta, mushrooms, cauliflower, olive
oil, grated Romano, mozzarella, provolone, herbs, spices and
sauce. Mix well. Cover with foil and bake casserole 30 minutes.
Uncover and bake another 5 minutes. Serve hot. Garnish with
sprigs of parsley.

ELBOWS WITH POTATOES AND BASIL

Serves 4-6

A nice, starchy, satisfying combination tinged with basil.

2 cups grated Pecorino Romano	**2 tablespoons dried parsley**
□	□
1/2 cup olive oil	**2 cups tomato sauce**
2 onions, minced	**1 teaspoon salt**
4 medium potatoes, quartered	**1/2 teaspoon pepper**
3 cloves garlic, finely minced	**1/4 teaspoon oregano**
2 tablespoons fresh basil, or 2	□
teaspoons dried	**1 pound elbow pasta**

In a large skillet gently warm olive oil. Add chopped onions, potatoes, garlic, basil and parsley. Saute, stirring frequently, until onions are transparent, about 5 minutes. Add tomato sauce, salt and pepper and oregano.

Cover and simmer over low heat for 20 minutes, or until potatoes are tender when pierced with a knife. Stir occasionally to prevent sticking.

While sauce simmers, bring 4 quarts water to a rollicking boil. Stir in pasta and cook until al dente, about 7 minutes. Drain and place in a deep bowl. Stir in potato mixture.

Serve at once and pass the grated cheese.

CALZONES WITH CHEESE AND PESTO

Serves 6   *Bake at 450*

Too delicious for words! There are many variations of calzones. Look for another one in the poultry chapter.

Dough
   1-1/2 teaspoons baking yeast   1/4 cup olive oil
   1 cup lukewarm water   ☐
   1 teaspoon honey   3 cups whole wheat flour
                                       1 teaspoon salt

Sprinkle yeast over warm water and honey. Stir to dissolve. Let mixture stand 5 minutes, or until yeast is foamy. Stir in olive oil.

Whirl flour and salt together using the steel blade of a food processor. With machine running, add yeast mixture through the feed tube.

Process until dough is smooth and cleans the sides of the workbowl, about 30 seconds. Add a little more water (a teaspoonful at a time) if dough will not form a ball, or a bit more flour if dough seems sticky. (Dough will be somewhat sticky until after first rise.) "Knead" 15-20 seconds. Place dough in bowl. Cover with plastic wrap or a shower cap and let rise until doubled in bulk, about 30 minutes.

Prepare filling while dough rises.

Filling
   2 cups ricotta   2 cups pesto
   2 cups grated cheese,   2 teaspoons dried basil
      pepperjack or mozzarella

Mix filling ingredients together well.

Final Preparation

Preheat oven to 450 degrees.

Punch down risen dough. Divide into 6 pieces and using a rolling pin, roll out in rounds 1/4-inch thick. Place 1/6 filling onto one side of each calzone. Fold empty half over and pinch edges together to seal filling. Prick to allow steam to escape.

Bake 15-20 minutes, or until calzones are crisp and lightly browned.

SPAGHETTI MUSHROOM MARINARA

Serves 4

This one is for mushroom lovers!

1/2 cup olive oil
8 cloves garlic, minced
□
2 cups tomato sauce
1 pound mushrooms, thickly
  sliced
1/4 teaspoon thyme

1/4 teaspoon oregano
1/4 teaspoon basil
1/4 teaspoon paprika
1 teaspoon black pepper
□
1 pound pasta
1 cup grated Pecorino
  Romano

Gently warm olive oil in a skillet or pot with a cover and saute garlic until aromatic. Add tomato sauce and mushrooms, together with herbs and spices. Cover and simmer 15 minutes.

While sauce simmers, bring 4 quarts water to a boil. Add pasta and cook until al dente, firm to the tooth, about 7 minutes. Drain and place back in pot. Pour sauce over and toss.

Place pasta on plates to serve and pass the Romano!

Grain and Bean
Main Dishes

BEAN AND GRAIN MAIN DISHES

Bean and grain dishes used to be thought suitable only for vegetarians. Or tasty ONLY if smothered in melted cheese. However, the rest of us are catching onto the fact that there's a whole world of ethnic cooking based on beans and grains, without cheese. There are over 7,000 varieties of legumes from around the world. We've only begun to scratch the surface in our kitchen.

Legumes or dried beans may well be the nutritional stars of the plant world. Low in fat and high in the kind of fiber that lowers cholesterol, they also contain components which are protective against cancer. When combined with grains, nuts, or seeds, they are an excellent protein source. What a delicious way to stay healthy!

These recipes freeze beautifully.

BLACK BEAN, CORN, AND SWEET POTATO STEW

Serves 6

Satisfying, easy to prepare. Serve with crusty brown bread and a green salad. Mangoes and berries would make a light dessert.

2 sweet potatoes, cubed	1 teaspoon basil
☐	1 teaspoon oregano
2 tablespoons olive oil	2 teaspoons salt
1 large onion, chopped	1/2 teaspoon cayenne pepper
4 cloves garlic, minced	☐
2 green peppers, chopped	3 cups cooked black beans
1 jalapeno pepper, seeded and	☐
finely minced	2 cups corn kernels, fresh
1 cup diced tomatoes	or frozen
1/4 cup dried parsley	

Steam sweet potato in 2 cups water until tender, but not over cooked. Drain and set aside.

Gently warm olive oil in a large skillet. Saute onion and garlic until onion is soft, about 5 minutes. Add peppers, tomato, parsley, herbs, salt and cayenne. Saute another 5 minutes.

Add sweet potatoes, black beans and corn to skillet. Cover and simmer stew until hot, 10 minutes. If stew starts to stick or burn, add a few tablespoons water.

Gently stir to mix. Taste, adjust seasonings, cover pot, and let stew stand 10 minutes for flavors to blend.

KIDNEY BEAN STEW WITH MILLET PILAF

Serves 6

Millet, an important grain in Indian and African cooking, has a pleasant, nutty flavor. Here it goes Italian!

1-1/2 cups millet	**1 jalapeno pepper, seeded, and**
3 cups water	**minced**
1/2 teaspoon salt	□
□	**1 teaspoon basil**
2 tablespoons olive oil	**1 teaspoon oregano**
2 onions, chopped	**3 cups cooked kidney beans**
4 carrots, sliced	**2 cups diced tomatoes**
1 red bell pepper, diced	**salt and pepper to taste**
1 green bell pepper, diced	**chopped parsley for garnish**

Toast millet in a dry saucepan over medium heat for 5 minutes, stirring constantly. Grains will brown slightly and begin to pop. Add water and salt, and bring to a boil. Cover saucepan and turn down heat. Simmer millet 30 minutes, until water has been absorbed.

Meanwhile, prepare stew. Gently warm oil in a large skillet. Saute onions, carrots, and peppers. Cover and cook 15 minutes, or until carrots are tender. Stir from time to time. Add herbs, cooked beans and tomatoes. Taste and adjust seasoning.

Place millet on each plate and spoon kidney bean mixture in the center. Garnish with chopped parsley.

Alternatively, millet and kidney bean mixture may be stirred together and served in bowls.

FAVA - MIDDLE EASTERN YELLOW SPLIT PEAS

Serves 12

There's something luscious about the combination of yellow split peas with garlic, olive oil and cumin.

4 cups yellow split peas
□
1/2 cup olive oil
1 large onion, chopped
4 cloves garlic, minced

1/2 teaspoon cayenne pepper
1/2 teaspoon cumin
1 teaspoon salt
1 teaspoon black pepper
□
chopped parsley for garnish

Using a mesh colander, rinse yellow split peas. Place in heavy pot with water to cover by 3 inches. Simmer on low until peas are tender, about an hour. Check and add water if necessary to prevent mixture from sticking.

Gently warm olive oil in a large skillet and saute onion and garlic. When split peas are soft and mushy, add to skillet. Stir until onions and garlic are well incorporated and then add remaining seasonings to taste.

Serve garnished with parsley.

Fava may be served like houmous, with pita and vegetables, or it may be used as an accompaniment to fish, chicken or meat instead of potatoes or rice.

INDIAN PLATTER

Serves 12

An exotic, Indian sampler with three entrees served side-by-side. Garnish with lemon slices and parsley.

Cauliflower with Basmati Rice

1 cup Basmati rice
2 cups water
□
2 tablespoons olive oil
1 teaspoon cumin seeds
1 tablespoon coriander seeds

1/2 teaspoon hot pepper flakes
1 teaspoon turmeric
2 tablespoons water
1 large head cauliflower broken into florets
salt, optional

Bring water to a boil, add rice and lower heat. Simmer covered for 45 minutes, while remainder of meal is being prepared.

Gently warm olive oil in a skillet. Add cumin, coriander, hot pepper flakes, turmeric, water and cauliflower. Cover and cook on low until cauliflower is tender. Add salt, if desired, to taste. Toss in cooked Basmati rice.

Indian Spinach

2 pounds spinach, finely chopped
4 tablespoons olive oil
4 cloves garlic, finely minced
1 teaspoon cumin

1 teaspoon chili powder
1 teaspoon coriander
1 teaspoon lemon juice
1 teaspoon salt

Gently warm olive oil in a skillet and stir in garlic and all spices and seasoning. Saute 2 minutes. Add spinach. Stir and cook until spinach is hot.

Lentils with Curry Sauce

2 cups green lentils

4 cups water

1 cup curry sauce

lemon to taste

salt and pepper to
taste

Bring water to a boil, add lentils and cook 15 minutes, or until lentils are tooth-tender, but not mushy. Add curry sauce, lemon, salt and pepper to taste.

To serve, place some of each entree on dinner plates. Or, put each entree on a serving platter and let people help themselves buffet style.

Curry Sauce, about 6 cups

1/4 cup olive oil

8-10 pasilla or poblano whole
dried red chiles

8 cloves garlic

1 large Spanish onion, quartered

2 tablespoons lemon juice

2 teaspoons curry powder

2 teaspoons salt

4 cups tomato sauce

In a large skillet, gently warm olive oil. Add dried chiles, stirring constantly for 5 minutes. Spoon chiles onto cutting board to cool. Cut stems and tops off and shake out most of the seeds. (Heat is in the seeds, so for a hot sauce, leave more in. Poblano and pasilla chiles are not hot, HOT peppers.)

Using the steel blade of a food processor, blend peppers, garlic and onion, together with lemon juice, curry powder, salt and tomato sauce. Scrape sauce back into skillet with a rubber spatula. Simmer 10 minutes.

Remove the one cup of sauce needed for this recipe and refrigerate or freeze the rest for future use. Curry sauce keeps for two months under refrigeration.

VEGETARIAN CHILI

Makes 8 cups to serve 6

Love chili? You'll love this! Serve this way, or over steamed brown rice. Blended, this chili makes a superb filling in tortillas for burritos. Use a dollop to accompany turkey tacos.

6 cups cooked beans - pinto, kidney, red beans, chickpeas, black beans -- all are good, mix and match

□

2 tablespoons olive oil
2 large onions, chopped
4 garlic cloves, minced
2 tablespoons chili powder
2 teaspoons ground cumin

□

1 pound carrots, halved lengthwise and sliced
2 cups diced tomatoes
1 green pepper, diced
1 red pepper, diced
1 jalapeno pepper, seeded and minced fine

□

1 teaspoon salt
1/2 teaspoon oregano

Gently warm olive oil in a soup kettle and saute onion and garlic until onion is softened. Add chili powder and cumin and stir 1 minute. Add carrots, diced tomatoes with their liquid, and peppers. Cover and simmer chili until carrots are tender, stirring occasionally, about 10 minutes.

Add beans to pot and simmer chili, covered, 15 minutes without stirring. Turn off heat, add salt and oregano, and mix chili so carrots are well-distributed. Cover pot again and let chili stand 30 minutes to give flavors a chance to blend.

Taste, adjust seasoning and serve.

TOFU EN SALSA VERDE WITH ADZUKI BEANS

Serves 6

Japanese beans and tofu with a spicy Mexican sauce!

1 pound tomatillos, husked
1 small onion
2 cloves garlic, minced
1 tablespoon dried parsley
1 chile chipotle
□
2 pounds firm tofu, cubed

3 tablespoons lime juice
□
3 cups cooked or canned and
**   rinsed adzuki beans**
□
parsley or cilantro for garnish
salt to taste

Place husked tomatillos in a saucepan with 1/2-inch deep water. Bring to a boil. Reduce heat and cover pot. Cook 10 minutes, or until tomatillos are tender. Drain and cool.

Place tomatillos, onion, garlic, parsley and chile in blender or food processor and puree.

Place sauce in a pot and simmer gently, uncovered, 15 minutes. Add tofu and lime juice. Let stand 15 minutes. Taste, adjust seasoning, cover pot and simmer another 5.

Spoon tofu and salsa verde onto plates. Depress the center and place 1/2 cup adzuki beans in depression. Garnish with a sprig of parsley or cilantro and serve immediately.

MID-EAST MUD - LENTILS WITH BULGUR

Serves 6

From the Middle East. Lentils and bulgur thicken as they cool. May be eaten hot or cold. Looks like mud, but tastes great!

Garnish with chopped hard-boiled eggs and sliced scallions.

1 cup uncooked lentils
5 cups water
□
1/3 cup olive oil
2 large onions, chopped

1 teaspoon salt
1/4 teaspoon black pepper
1/3 cup unsoaked bulgur
□
scallions and hard-boiled egg, sliced, for garnish

Rinse lentils and place in a pot with 5 cups water. Cover and bring to a boil. Lower heat and simmer 15 minutes.

Gently warm olive oil in a skillet. Saute chopped onions until golden, about 7 minutes.

Add onions, scrapings from the pan, salt and pepper, and bulgur to lentils. Cover and cook 25 minutes, stirring occasionally.

Let stand 15 minutes, taste, adjust seasoning, and serve garnished with scallions and hard-boiled egg slices.

GREEK STEW WITH POTATOES, TOMATOES PEPPER AND TOFU

Serves 8

A terrific Greek stew with tofu instead of fish.

2 pounds firm tofu, cubed and marinated in 1-1/2 tbs. lemon juice
□
8 medium baking potatoes, cut lengthwise into spears
□
1/2 cup olive oil
1 large onion, chopped
2 large garlic cloves, minced
2 green peppers, sliced

4 cups tomatoes, diced
1/2 cup fresh parsley, chopped
1 teaspoon oregano
4 bay leaves
1 tablespoon paprika
1 teaspoon black pepper
□
1/2 cup cider vinegar
□
salt to taste

Cube tofu and marinate in lemon juice while preparing the remainder of the dish.

Steam potatoes until tender, about 15-20 minutes.

While potatoes steam, gently warm olive oil. Saute onion and garlic until softened, about 5 minutes. Add green pepper and saute another few minutes. Add tomatoes, parsley, oregano, bay leaves, paprika and black pepper, and simmer, uncovered, 15 minutes, or until potatoes are ready.

Add cider vinegar, steamed potatoes, and tofu to sauce. Cover, turn off heat, and let stew stand 10 minutes to give the flavors a chance to blend. Taste, adjust seasoning and serve.

POTATO BURRITOS CON SALSA VERDE

Serves 9   *Bake at 350*

An unusual filling for burritos, yummy nonetheless!

Salsa Verde
- **1 pound tomatillos, husked**
- **3 jalapenos, seeded**
- **1 cup parsley or cilantro**
- **1 large onion**
- **salt and pepper to taste**

Tortilla Stuffing
- **4 tablespoons olive oil**
- **2 large onions, diced**
- **6 cloves garlic, minced**
- **2 green bell peppers, halved and sliced in strips**
- **☐**
- **1 teaspoon chili powder**
- **1 teaspoon oregano**
- **3 large potatoes, julienned**
- **1 pound soft or silken tofu**
- **salt to taste**
- **☐**
- **18 flour tortillas**
- **☐**
- **sesame seeds for garnish**
- **sprigs of cilantro or parsley for garnish**

Place husked tomatillos in a saucepan with water to cover. Bring to a boil and simmer 5 minutes. Drain into a colander. Using a food processor or blender, blend tomatillos with jalapenos, parsley or cilantro and onion. Taste and add salt if desired.

Gently warm olive oil in a large skillet. Saute diced onions, garlic and green peppers until peppers are brightly colored and onion is soft, about 4 minutes. Stir in chili powder, oregano, and potato. Cover skillet. Cook on low just until potatoes are tooth-tender. If necessary, add a spoonful of water to prevent from burning. Stir often to prevent from sticking.

When potatoes are soft, add tofu, which will crumble as you stir dish.

Taste and add more pepper and salt if desired.

Preheat oven to 350 degrees.

Place tortillas on a plate or flat surface. Spread a spoonful of filling in a strip just above the center. Roll tortilla tightly and place seam side down in a serving dish. When all tortillas are filled and rolled, bake for 10 minutes.

To serve, cover with salsa verde and garnish with sesame seeds and sprigs of cilantro or parsley.

LATKES

Serves 4

Potato pancakes -- potatoes and onions sizzling in oil -- made at Chanukah taste as wonderful as they smell. Start a second batch as soon as the first is off the griddle or out of the frying pan. People eat their weight in latkes!

6 medium potatoes, scrubbed but UNPEELED
3 onions, quartered
1 unbeaten egg

1 teaspoon salt
1 teaspoon black pepper
peanut oil for frying

Grate potatoes and onions with the fine shredding disk of a food processor. (Watch the knuckles if you grate by hand.)

Mix grated potatoes and onions, egg, salt and pepper in a bowl. Drop batter by large spoonfuls into a frying pan with hot oil barely deep enough to cover latkes, or make them on a well buttered pancake griddle heated for griddlecakes. Pour a small amount of oil around each pancake as it sizzles on the griddle. Brown latkes on both sides for either method.

The batter will become soupy in the bowl as it stands. Rather than draining or squeezing liquid out, or adding flour to absorb it, just stir it back into batter before using.

Drain latkes on absorbent paper and serve hot - plain, with applesauce, or sour cream.

AMY'S SPICY STIR-FRY WITH PEANUT SAUCE

Serves 8

Spicy and sweet, this dish is a complete meal and takes only about half an hour to prepare.

Sauce:
- *1/2 cup peanut butter*
- *1/2 cup warm water*
- *3/8 cup tamari*
- *1/4 cup rice wine vinegar*

- *2 tablespoons toasted sesame oil*
- *1 tablespoon crushed red pepper*

- *1/2 cup toasted sesame oil*
- *1/2 cup raw peanuts or cashews*
- *1 pound raw, boned chicken*
  - *or*
- *1 pound tofu, cubed*
- *1 teaspoon crushed red pepper*
- *2 tablespoons tamari*
- *4 cups broccoli florets*
- *3 carrots thinly sliced*

- *1 large onion, chopped*
- *4 cloves garlic, crushed*
- *3 cups mung bean sprouts*
- *2 firm bananas, sliced*
- *1/4 cup unsweetened dry coconut*
- *2 pounds soba noodles*

Make sauce by blending peanut butter, water, tamari, vinegar, sesame oil, and red pepper. Set aside.

Boil water for noodles. Prepare remaining ingredients for stir-fry. Place noodles in boiling water when ready to fry.

To stir-fry, heat 1/4 cup sesame oil in a wok or deep fry pan. Add nuts, chicken or tofu, pepper and tamari. Stir-fry until chicken is done and nuts brown. Remove from pan and set aside. Heat remaining oil and add broccoli and carrots. Cook 2 minutes, then add onion and garlic. Cook another 5 minutes, until onion is translucent. Add sliced banana, chicken, nuts and sprouts.

Serve on soba noodles with peanut sauce and coconut.

BARLEY WITH CHESTNUTS AND DRIED FRUIT

Serves 4

Dandelion greens, swiss chard, spinach or arugula are a fine accompaniment to this dish. Dried fruit makes an unexpected counterpoint to barley and chile peppers.

1 cup pearled barley	1 cup peeled chestnuts
2-1/2 cups water	1/2 cup figs
☐	1/2 cup apricots
2 teaspoons black pepper	1/2 cup prunes
1 teaspoon salt	1 dried chile pepper
1-1/2 teaspoons olive oil	1 cup water

Bring water to a boil. Stir in barley, lower heat, cover pot and simmer until water has been absorbed and barley is tender, about 50 minutes. When done, stir in black pepper, salt, and olive oil.

While the barley is cooking, place peeled chestnuts in a 2-quart pot with fruit, chile pepper and water. Bring to a boil. Cover pot, lower heat and simmer 30 minutes. All the liquid should be absorbed and the fruit soft, but still in large pieces.

Turn barley out onto plates and make an indentation in the middle. Spoon fruit into indentation. Sprinkle more black pepper to taste over the fruit.

BARLEY WITH RUSSIAN WALNUT SAUCE
AND COLORED PEPPERS

Serves 8-10

Barley is one of the oldest grains on earth. Walnut sauce is wonderful over any grain, or even over pasta, fish or poultry.

Walnut Sauce
- 2 heaping cups walnuts
- 1 teaspoon salt
- 4 cloves garlic
- 1 teaspoon coriander
- 1/2 teaspoon fenugreek seeds
- 1/4 teaspoon turmeric
- 1/2 teaspoon paprika
- 6 teaspoons cider vinegar
- 1-1/2 cups water

- 9 cups water
- 3 cups barley
- ☐
- 2 tablespoons olive oil
- 2 red bell peppers, sliced
- 2 green bell peppers, sliced
- 2 yellow bell peppers, sliced
- ☐
- parsley for garnish
- walnut halves for garnish

Using the steel blade of a food processor, blend walnuts, salt, garlic, coriander, fenugreek, turmeric and paprika until smooth. Run the machine and drizzle in vinegar and enough water to make a sauce the consistency of light cream. Transfer sauce to a bowl, cover and refrigerate for at least an hour, allowing the flavors to blend.

In the meantime, bring water to a boil and add barley. Lower heat, cover pot and simmer 50 minutes, or until barley is tender.

In a skillet, warm olive oil and saute peppers until they begin to wilt but are still brilliant in color.

To serve, mound barley on individual plates. Place peppers to the side, top with walnut sauce and garnish plates with parsley and walnut pieces.

VEGETABLE PAELLA WITH ABORIO RICE

Serves 6

Aborio rice, an Italian short-grain rice typically used in risotto, together with vegetables, makes a colorful dish. Short-grain brown rice works beautifully too.

1/2 cup water
2 carrots, halved lengthwise
    and sliced
1/4 pound green beans,
    cut into 2" lengths
    □
4 tablespoons olive oil
1 large onion, chopped
6 cloves garlic, minced
1 large green and red,
    pepper chopped
1 jalapeno pepper, minced
2 cups aborio rice

2 cups chopped tomatoes
1/4 teaspoon saffron
3 cups water
1 teaspoon salt
1/2 teaspoon cayenne pepper
    □
1 cup slivered almonds
1/2 cup dried parsley
1 cup green peas
2 zucchini, halved and sliced
    □
soy granules, optional
whole almonds, for garnish

Steam carrots in 1/2 cup water until crisp-tender. Place in colander and cool under water. Drain. Set aside. Steam green beans the same way. Cool under water, drain and set aside.

Gently warm olive oil in skillet and saute onion, garlic, and peppers 3 minutes. Add rice and stir until translucent, a minute or two. Add tomatoes and saffron and simmer 5 minutes. Add water, salt and cayenne, and bring paella to a boil. Cover and simmer 40 minutes, until rice is tooth-tender.

Stir in slivered almonds, parsley, peas, carrots, string beans and zucchini. Cover skillet and let paella stand for a few minutes. If rice is wet, stir in several tablespoons soy granules to absorb excess moisture.

POTATO KIBBI

Serves 8   *Bake at 400*

A Middle-Eastern specialty. Serve with green beans, olives, fresh tomatoes, sliced cucumbers, and pita bread. Kibbi also may be served as an appetizer.

1-1/2 cups bulgur
1-1/2 cups boiling water
2 teaspoons salt
□
4 small-medium potatoes,
   quartered and steamed
   until soft

1 tablespoon basil
1/8 teaspoon cinnamon
1/8 teaspoon pepper
1 small onion, grated
1 teaspoon salt
□
2 large onions, julienned
2/3 cup olive oil

Pour boiling water over bulgur. Sprinkle with salt and stir once. Let stand for 20 minutes.

While bulgur is soaking, steam potatoes with water until tender, about 20 minutes. Drain and mash with potato masher or a wooden spoon. Mix basil, cinnamon, pepper, grated onion and salt into potatoes. Add bulgur and knead into soft dough. (The mixture will not stick if your hands are wet.) If the dough does not stick together, add 1/4 cup potato flour.

Place julienned onions in the bottom of an 11x17 baking pan. Pour over 1/3 cup olive oil. Place the potato bulgur mixture evenly on top - use your hands to pat out - and cut into diamond shapes about 1/2" deep. Pour the remaining oil on top and bake at 400 degrees until golden brown, about 25 minutes.

WILD RICE WITH SHITAKE MUSHROOMS

Serves 6, or 12 as a side dish

Shitake mushrooms add to the robust, earthy flavor of wild rice. An excellent stuffing or side dish accompaniment to fish or poultry.

2 cups raw wild rice
2 teaspoons salt
7 cups water
□
1/4 cup olive oil
1 large onion, coarsely chopped
3 large ribs celery, diced
2 medium carrots, coarsely chopped

1 teaspoon leaf marjoram, crumbled
1/2 teaspoon rosemary
1/2 teaspoon thyme
1 teaspoon black pepper
□
1/4 pound dried Shitake mushrooms, soaked overnight and thinly sliced

In a large, heavy saucepan, combine wild rice with salt and 7 cups water and bring to a boil over moderate heat. Reduce flame and simmer, partially covered, until rice has popped and grains are tender, but slightly chewy, about 55 minutes. Drain well and set aside.

Meanwhile, in a skillet, gently warm olive oil and add onion and celery and cook, stirring frequently, until limp and golden, about 10 minutes. Add carrots, marjoram, rosemary, thyme and pepper and reduce heat to low. Cover and cook 10 minutes. Using a slotted spoon, transfer vegetables to a large bowl.

Add mushrooms to skillet and increase heat to moderately high. Cook, stirring for 5 minutes. Add mushrooms to bowl of vegetables. Add hot wild rice and toss. Taste, adjust seasoning and serve.

MILLET IN A NEST OF VEGETABLES WITH TOMATO COULIS

Serves 4

Millet with colorful, sauteed vegetables and a spicy tomato coulis.

Vegetables and Millet

2 cups millet	1 yellow crookneck squash,
4 cups water	julienned
1 teaspoon salt	☐
☐	1 tablespoon olive oil
1 stalk celery, julienned	2 cloves garlic, crushed
1 onion, diced	1 teaspoon black pepper
1 large carrot, julienned	salt to taste
1 large zucchini, julienned	

Tomato Coulis

2 cups tomatoes, diced	1 tablespoon cider vinegar
2 cloves garlic, minced	1 teaspoon dried basil
1 teaspoon red pepper flakes	salt and pepper to taste

Bring water and salt to a boil. Stir in millet, lower heat, cover pot and simmer 45 minutes.

Steam vegetables until crisp-tender. Warm olive oil in a skillet. Add garlic and stir. Stir in vegetables and black pepper just to coat with oil. Season with salt, if desired. Set aside.

In a pan, simmer tomatoes, garlic, red pepper flakes, vinegar and basil 15 minutes, or until coulis thickens. Adjust seasoning.

Mound 1 cup millet on each plate. Place vegetables decoratively around millet. Make a depression in the center and spoon on tomato coulis. Serve immediately.

RICE PILAF WITH SPINACH AND CANNELLINI

Serves 4

Sun-dried tomatoes, rice, white kidney beans and Pecorino Romano. Serve fresh apricots or peaches for dessert.

1 tablespoon olive oil
1 onion, chopped
4 cloves garlic, minced
1-1/2 cups brown Basmati rice
3 cups water or vegetable broth
□
3 cups cooked cannellini beans
  (white kidneys), or 3 cups
  canned, rinsed and drained

8 cups fresh spinach, chopped
1/2 cup freshly grated Pecorino
  Romano cheese
1 teaspoon black pepper
salt, if desired, to taste
□
3 tablespoons pine nuts
1/4 cup oil-packed sun-dried
  tomatoes, sliced thinly

Gently warm olive oil in a large skillet. Saute onion and garlic until onion is golden, about 5-7 minutes. Reduce heat and stir in rice until opaque, about 3 minutes. Add water and bring to boil. Cover skillet and simmer until rice is tender, about 45 minutes.

When rice is cooked, mix in beans, spinach, Romano and black pepper. Cover and continue cooking until thoroughly heated, usually several minutes.

Taste and adjust seasoning. Remove pilaf to serving platter and garnish with pine nuts and sun-dried tomatoes.

MEXICAN TAMALE PEPPERS

Serves 12   *Bake at 350*

A filling so flavorful, it needs no cheese! Serve with a marinated vegetable salad and honeydew melon for dessert.

1/4 cup olive oil
4 cloves garlic, chopped
2 large onions, chopped
    □
3 tablespoons chili powder
2 teaspoons ground cumin
2 cups masa harina, or very fine
    cornmeal

6 cups chopped tomatoes,
    with liquid
1 teaspoon salt
    □
4 cups cooked pink beans
1 pound corn kernels
    □
12 large green bell peppers

Gently warm olive oil in a large skillet. Saute onion and garlic until soft, about 5 minutes. Add chili and cumin and then stir in tomatoes, masa harina, and salt. Cook, stirring until mixture is thick, about 5 minutes. Stir in beans and corn. Stir another 5 minutes.

Preheat oven to 350 degrees.

Slice tops from peppers, remove seeds and tough inner ribs. Spoon cornmeal mixture into peppers and place them upright in a baking dish. Cover pan with foil and bake peppers 40 minutes, or until tender.

If desired, serve peppers with a spoonful of salsa on top.

FELAFEL

Makes 36 felafel balls, or 12 servings

Sold on street corners in the Middle East, felafel is usually served inside pita bread with shredded lettuce, chopped tomatoes, and tahini sauce.

*2-1/2 cups chickpeas soaked
    overnight
1/4 cup buckwheat groats
3 cloves garlic
2 eggs
handful parsley*

*2 teaspoons salt
1/4 teaspoon cayenne pepper
2 teaspoons cumin
1 teaspoon oregano
vegetable oil for frying*

Using the steel blade of a food processor, blend ingredients until they are moist and resemble fine breadcrumbs. If batter will not hold together when pressed between fingers, mix in water, 1 tablespoon at a time, until it will. Allow to stand for 1/2 hour.

Heat oil in fry pan. Make balls the size of walnuts. Drop into sizzling oil with a slotted spoon. Be careful not to cause oil to splash. Fry felafel to a deep brown.

Serve immediately with toothpicks as an appetizer or place three felafel inside each pita with tahini sauce and lettuce and tomato.

Tahini Sauce

1/4 cup tahini	*2 cloves garlic*
1/4 cup lemon juice	*1 teaspoon salt*
1/2 cup water	

Using the steel blade of the food processor again, or a blender, blend ingredients until smooth and no pieces of garlic remain.   Add   more   water   if   necessary   to   reach   pouring consistency. Some people prefer tahini sauce very liquidy, others want a sauce which is almost thick enough to use as a dip.

INDIAN QUINOA WITH FIGS AND CARDAMOM

Serves 6

Garnished with peanuts or cashew pieces, quinoa, figs and cardamom are wonderfully fragrant.

2 tablespoons olive oil
2 onions, chopped
4 cloves garlic, finely minced
1 red pepper, cut into strips
  □
1/2 head cauliflower, broken into florets
4 carrots, diced
1-1/2 cups quinoa
4 cardamom pods

1/4 teaspoon cumin
1 teaspoon salt
1/2 teaspoon black pepper
3 cups water
  □
1 cup whole dried figs
  □
1 cup cashew pieces or peanuts for garnish

Gently warm olive oil in a large skillet. Saute onions, garlic, and pepper until fragrant and onion is soft, about 5 minutes.

Add cauliflower, carrots, quinoa, cardamom pods, cumin, and salt and pepper. Stir 3-5 minutes. Add water and simmer, covered, for 10 minutes. Turn off heat, add figs and leave skillet covered.

Allow quinoa to stand off heat for 10 minutes and fork up just before serving. Garnish with cashew pieces or peanuts.

EGGPLANT, PASTA AND CHICK PEA STEW

Serves 8

Beans and pasta, topped with an eggplant sauce make a satisfying combination.

4 tablespoons olive oil
2 large onions, chopped
6 cloves garlic, minced
1 green pepper, chopped
☐
1 large eggplant, peeled and cubed in 1" pieces
☐
2 cups chopped tomatoes
1-1/2 teaspoons salt

1/2 teaspoon black pepper
1/2 teaspoon oregano
1/2 teaspoon cayenne pepper (optional)
☐
2 cups chick peas, cooked or canned (if canned, drained)
☐
2 cups elbow macaroni of your choice

Gently warm olive oil in a skillet. Saute onion, garlic and green pepper for 5 minutes. Add eggplant and saute another 10 minutes, stirring occasionally. Add tomatoes, seasonings, herbs, and chick peas to stew. Cover and simmer 30 minutes. Watch carefully. If stew appears to be sticking, add a little boiling water.

While stew simmers, bring a large pot of water to a boil and cook pasta until al dente, about 7 minutes. Drain pasta and stir into stew. Taste, adjust seasoning and serve hot or cold.

SPICY STUFFED EGGPLANT

Serves 6   *Bake at 375*

A colorful, fragrant twist to a classic. Potatoes and tofu replace the heavy meat and cheese filling that is often used. Serve with a red leaf lettuce salad and follow with fruit of the season.

3 medium eggplants	1/2 teaspoon cayenne
4 cups cubed potatoes	1/4 teaspoon cloves
1 pound silken tofu	☐
☐	2 medium carrots, diced
2 tablespoons olive oil	1 tablespoon lemon juice
4 garlic cloves, minced	1 green pepper, diced
2 cups chopped onions	1 cup string beans, in 2" pieces
2 teaspoons ground cumin	☐
1 teaspoon tumeric	2 cups cooked chickpeas

Slice eggplants in half lengthwise, leaving stems on. Place cut side down on an oiled baking sheet. Cover and bake at 375 degrees until tender, about 30-40 minutes. While eggplant is baking, boil potatoes until tender. Drain. Using a food processor, blend potatoes with tofu.

Gently warm olive oil in a skillet and saute onions, garlic and spices until onions are translucent. Add carrots and lemon juice. Simmer 5 minutes before adding pepper and string beans to cook an additional 5 minutes. Combine vegetables with potato.

Turn baked eggplant halves over in baking pan. With a fork or spoon, mash pulp, taking care not to break the skin. Push aside some of the pulp, making a hollow in each half. Divide filling and mound on each half. Bake covered 15 minutes, then uncovered for an additional 15-20 minutes.

Serve with chickpeas on the side. Sprinkle with black pepper.

ITALIAN EGGPLANT WITH NUTS AND SEEDS

Serves 4   *Bake at 350*

This recipe was given to us by Barbara Shoemaker and Bob Larkin who adapted it from a dish made by Carol Priest, a friend of theirs from California. Barbara says the secret is the vinegar.

1/2 cup cashew pieces
1/2 cup sunflower seeds
        ☐
1 medium eggplant, sliced
    in 1/2 inch slices
1/2 cup olive oil
1 onion, chopped
2 ribs celery, diced

1 large green pepper, chopped
3 tablespoons dried parsley
3 cloves garlic, minced
        ☐
1 cup tomato sauce
1/3 cup wine vinegar
pepper to taste

Preheat oven to 350 degrees. Roast cashews and sunflower seeds on a cookie sheet for 10 minutes. Remove to cool.

Bake sliced eggplant until tender, about 15 minutes. Cut into cubes. (This step can be eliminated. Eggplant can be cubed and sauteed along with remaining vegetables. Doing so will result in a softer, wetter eggplant.)

Gently warm olive oil in a skillet. Saute onion, celery, green pepper, parsley and garlic about 5 minutes.

Add eggplant, tomato sauce and vinegar. Simmer, covered, for 15 minutes. Add pepper to taste. Stir in toasted cashews and sunflower seeds.

Serve over steamed brown rice.

Poultry Main Dishes

POULTRY MAIN DISHES

We love ground chicken and turkey. Lower in fat and calories than ground beef, they are easily substituted with great results. Try sheesh kebabs or turkey tacos and see for yourself!

Store raw poultry no longer than 1-2 days in the refrigerator. Once cooked, use within 3-4 days. Frozen poultry can be stored for 6-9 months.

Always wash poultry before using.

Instead of browning poultry in oil, we broil or bake it to achieve the same results, but without the additional fat.

CHICKEN TACOS

Makes 4 generous servings

Kids of ALL ages love these lighter tacos. If ground chicken is not available, substitute ground turkey.

2 tablespoons olive oil
1 large onion, chopped
4 cloves garlic, minced
☐
2 pounds ground chicken
☐
2 teaspoons cumin
2 teaspoons chili powder
2 jalapeno peppers, minced
1/2 teaspoon oregano

1/2 teaspoon thyme
1 cup tomato sauce
salt and pepper to taste
☐
corn tortillas
2 tomatoes, chopped
1 avocado, peeled and chopped
☐
2 cups vegetarian chili

Gently warm olive oil in a large skillet. Saute onions and garlic until onions begin to soften, about 2-3 minutes. Add chicken and saute until nicely browned.

Add spices, peppers and tomato sauce. Simmer 10 minutes. Taste and adjust seasoning.

Spoon taco mixture over a corn tortilla. Top with tomato and avocado. Accompany with a heaping spoonful of vegetarian chili on the side.

CHICKEN STEW WITH POTATOES AND TOMATOES

Serves 8   *Bake at 350*

A snap to prepare. Mix everything and pop into the oven!

**2 pounds boneless chicken
    breasts, skinless and cubed
16 small red potatoes, quartered
2 cups coarsely chopped fresh or
    canned tomatoes
6 cloves garlic, minced
1 teaspoon black pepper**

**2 teaspoons oregano
1 teaspoon thyme
1 teaspoon marjoram
1/4 cup olive oil
8 ounces mushrooms, sliced
    □
chopped parsley for garnish**

Preheat oven to 350 degrees.

Place chicken in an oven-proof casserole. Add potatoes, tomatoes, garlic, pepper, oregano, thyme, marjoram, olive oil and mushrooms. Stir to mix.

Bake, uncovered, 1 hour, or until potatoes are easily pierced with a knife. Baste casserole with its own sauce every 20 minutes. Remove from oven and sprinkle with parsley to serve.

MIDDLE-EASTERN TURKEY BURGERS

Serves 6

A favorite for informal entertaining with each guest putting together her/his own burger.

Turkey Burger

2 pounds ground turkey	**2 teaspoons cumin**
1 medium onion, minced	**1 teaspoon salt**
2 cloves garlic, minced	**1 teaspoon black pepper**
1/2 teaspoon oregano	**2 tablespoons rice, wheat or oat**
2 tablespoons dried parsley	**bran**

Tahini Dressing

1/2 cup sesame tahini	□
1/4 cup lemon juice	**2 tablespoons olive oil**
about 1/2 cup water to thin	**3 cups chopped tomatoes**
2 cloves garlic	□
	6 whole grain hamburger buns

Knead burgers together in a mixing bowl and shape. Grill or broil 4-5 minutes on each side.

Using the steel blade of a food processor or a blender, blend tahini, lemon, garlic and water. Dressing should be the consistency of heavy cream. If it is too thick, add a few more spoonfuls of water. Taste dressing and adjust seasoning.

Mix chopped tomatoes with a little olive oil.

To serve, place turkey burgers on bun. Spoon dressing and chopped tomatoes on top.

TURKEY SHEESH KEBABS

Serves 4

These spicy kebabs are excellent served over brown rice or inside pita at a cookout. Or try serving them with black beans and sweet potatoes for contrasting taste and color!

3 cloves garlic, minced	2 tablespoons lemon juice
1 medium onion, chopped	2 tablespoons dried parsley
1 pound ground turkey	1/2 teaspoon chili powder
1 pound soft tofu	1/2 teaspoon black pepper
1 tablespoon whole wheat flour	1/2 teaspoon red pepper
	salt to taste, optional

In a bowl combine garlic and onion with ground turkey, tofu, flour, lemon juice, and spices. Use your hands to knead the mixture.

Divide sheesh kebabs into 8 equal long, cigar-shaped burgers.

Broil or grill until lightly browned. Serve hot over rice.

Garnish with a sprig of parsley or watercress.

This makes a great turkey meatloaf. Pat into an ungreased bread pan and bake, uncovered, at 350 degrees for 1 hour.

CHICKEN CON MOLÉ VERDE

Serves 6-8   *Bake at 350*

Chicken with a deliciously fragrant Mexican sauce. Tomatillos are a Mexican paper-husked green tomato, which are easily grown in home gardens anywhere tomatoes can be grown! Serve with boiled rice or barley or millet.

3 pounds boneless chicken
1 large onion, chopped
6 garlic cloves, minced
1 teaspoon salt
   ☐
1/2 cup pumpkin seeds
   ☐
1-1/2 pounds tomatillos, husked

2 large dried ancho chiles
2 cloves garlic
1/4 cup dried parsley
   ☐
3 tablespoons olive oil
1/2 teaspoon salt
1/2 teaspoon cumin

Mix chicken with onion, garlic and salt. Bake in a 350 degree oven until chicken juice runs clear when meat is pierced with a knife, about 30 minutes.

To dry-roast pumpkin seeds, stir in a hot pan until lightly browned, 2-3 minutes. Cool slightly.

Place husked tomatillos in a saucepan with water to cover. Bring to a boil and cook 10 minutes. Drain and cool. Combine tomatillos, chiles, 2 cloves garlic, parsley and pumpkin seeds in a food processor. Blend until pumpkin seeds are finely ground.

Gently warm olive oil in a large skillet. Add pumpkin seed sauce. Simmer five minutes. Add chicken, remaining salt and cumin. Simmer uncovered 15 minutes. Spoon out over grain.

SPICY CHICKEN CURRY

Serves 12

Our favorite, sensual curry sauce. The sauce recipe makes about 6 cups, enough to use and enough to save in a glass jar in the refrigerator for last minute additions to fish, tofu, or beans.

Steamed green beans provide a crunch and color contrast when served as an accompaniment.

Sauce, about 6 cups

1/4 cup olive oil	2 tablespoons lemon juice
8-10 pasilla or poblano whole dried red chiles	2 teaspoons curry powder
	2 teaspoons salt
8 cloves garlic	4 cups tomato sauce
1 large Spanish onion, quartered	

4 pounds boneless chicken breasts or thighs with the skin removed, cut into bite-sized pieces

8 large steamed potatoes cut into chunks, or 6 cups cooked chickpeas, or 8 cups cooked Basmati rice

a green vegetable, such as string beans.

In a large skillet, gently warm olive oil. Add dried chiles, stirring constantly for 5 minutes. Spoon chiles onto cutting board to cool. Cut stems and tops off and shake out most of the seeds. (Heat is in the seeds, so for a hot sauce, leave more in. Poblano and pasilla chiles are not hot, HOT peppers.)

Using the steel blade of a food processor, blend peppers, garlic and onion, together with lemon juice, curry powder, salt and tomato sauce. Scrape sauce back into skillet with a rubber spatula. Simmer 10 minutes.

Leaving 2 cups sauce in skillet, remove 4 cups and refrigerate for future use. Curry sauce keeps for two months under refrigeration.

Add chicken to sauce and simmer over medium heat for 10 minutes. Cover skillet and cook another 30 minutes, or until poultry is thoroughly cooked and has had a chance to absorb the flavors. Add potatoes, chickpeas, or rice to skillet and mix well.

Alternatively, bake chicken and raw potatoes mixed with curry sauce, uncovered in oven until potatoes are soft and chicken is nice and brown, about 1-1/2 to 2 hours.

CHICKEN MOLÉ WITH ALMONDS AND SESAME

Serves 6

Molé without chocolate. Thanks to Gabrielle Matuz for the idea!

2 tablespoons olive oil
2 dried ancho peppers
1 dried pasilla pepper
□
1 large onion
6 cloves garlic
2 medium tomatoes
2 tablespoons almonds
2 tablespoons sesame seeds
1/2 teaspoon cloves

3 teaspoons pepper
1/4 teaspoon cinnamon
1 teaspoon salt
□
3 cups water
1-1/2 cups raw brown rice
□
1-1/2 pounds 1/2-inch thick
  chicken slices
sesame seeds to garnish

In a large skillet, gently warm olive oil. Add peppers and stir-fry 5 minutes. Remove peppers from oil and blend in a food processor. Strain to eliminate peel and seeds. Set pepper puree aside.

Using the food processor again, blend onion, garlic, tomato, almonds, sesame seeds and seasonings. Add mixture to same skillet and simmer 10 minutes. If necessary, add a little water to prevent burning. Add pepper puree. Simmer another 5 minutes.

While molé simmers, in a small pot, bring 3 cups water to a boil. Sir in rice. Cover pot, lower heat and simmer rice 45 minutes. Turn heat off and leave cover on until ready to use rice.

Add chicken to sauce in skillet. Cover and simmer 30 minutes. Taste and adjust seasoning. Serve chicken molé over rice. Sprinkle with sesame seeds for garnish.

SPANISH CHICKEN WITH FAKIN' BACON

Serves 8-10   *Bake at 350*

Inspired by paella, but simpler, with fewer ingredients.

3 pounds chicken thighs and drumsticks

☐

2 tablespoons olive oil
1 onion, diced
6 cloves garlic, minced
1 red bell pepper, diced
3 cups chopped tomatoes

☐

1-6 ounce package Fakin' Bacon,* diced

2 cups raw short-grain brown rice
4 cups boiling water
pinch saffron (about 3-4 threads)
2 teaspoons salt
2 teaspoons black pepper

☐

several sprigs fresh parsley
black olives

Preheat oven to 350 degrees.

To make the sauce, gently warm olive oil in a large skillet and saute onion, garlic, pepper and tomatoes until sauce thickens. Dice Fakin' Bacon and add to skillet. Saute another 5 minutes, stirring occasionally.

Spoon sauce into a large shallow baking pan or casserole dish. Add rice, saffron threads, salt and pepper, and stir until rice is coated. Pour boiling water into casserole and place chicken pieces over the top. Bake casserole, uncovered, 45 minutes, or until rice has absorbed all the liquid and dish is fragrant.

Serve garnished with parsley and olives.

*Fakin' Bacon is a soy product which has a smoky flavor. Use it in any recipe which calls for ham or bacon. You can find it in any natural food store. We love it in paella, bean soups, etc.

EASY CHICKEN CURRY

Serves 8

Serve on a bed of fluffy rice. Basmati rice is especially fragrant.

2 onions, quartered
4 cloves garlic
2 tablespoons lemon juice
1 teaspoon curry powder
1/2 teaspoon red pepper flakes
1 teaspoon salt
1/2 teaspoon ground ginger

1/2 cup tomato sauce or 1 large tomato
□
3 pounds chicken pieces with skin removed
□
4 cups cooked garbanzo beans

Using the steel blade of a food processor, blend onions, garlic, lemon juice, curry, red pepper, salt, ginger and tomato. Stop the machine once or twice to scrape down the sides of the workbowl with a rubber spatula.

Remove sauce to a fry pan and stir 3 minutes, until mixture begins to darken attractively. Add chicken and turn to coat. Cover fry pan and simmer chicken for an hour, stirring once or twice, or until tender. Add chickpeas and cook just until they are heated through.

Serve on a bed of rice garnished with a sprig of parsley or watercress.

As a variation, try tofu or shrimp. Adjust the cooking time accordingly - shrimp until they turn pink, tofu, until heated through.

INDIAN CHICKEN

Serves 8   *Bake at 400*

Flavorful, not spicy. Want more heat, add more red pepper!
Serve with millet or baked potatoes and a cucumber yogurt salad.

8 large garlic cloves
1 large onion, quartered
1 teaspoon ginger
1/2 teaspoon cumin
1 teaspoon chili powder
1/2 teaspoon salt
1/2 teaspoon each red and
black pepper

1/4 teaspoon ground
cardamom
□
1 3-4 pound chicken, cut into
serving pieces
1 lemon

Using the steel blade of a food processor, puree garlic and
onion together with spices. Stop the machine once or twice to
scrape down the sides of the workbowl with a rubber spatula.
When paste is smooth, coat chicken. Cover and marinate for
several hours, or overnight.

Before baking, make a number of small cuts in chicken and
squeeze lemon juice all over.

Roast chicken in a 400 degree oven for 1 hour. Baste several
times with pan juices.

CHICKEN WITH ALMONDS AND SNOW PEAS

Serves 4

From the Orient.   Flavors and textures unencumbered by cornstarch.

1/2 cup almonds
□
1 green pepper, chopped
2 onions, chopped
4 cloves garlic, minced
2 tablespoons sesame oil
□
2 cups boneless chicken pieces

4-ounce can sliced water chestnuts
1 pound Chinese snow peas, stringed
1/4 cup tamari soy sauce
□
4 cups cooked brown rice

Toast almonds in a 250 degree oven for 10 minutes. Set aside to cool.

Heat oil in wok or large frying pan. Saute green pepper, onions and garlic, stirring constantly. Add chicken and continue stirring 2 minutes. Add water chestnuts, snow peas and tamari. Stir-fry 2 minutes.

Place brown rice on individual serving plates and mound chicken and vegetables attractively in the middle. Sprinkle with toasted almonds and serve immediately.

LEMON CHICKEN

Serves 4

The combination of yogurt, lemon, and tomato gives this chicken a distinctive flavor and fragrance. Serve over bulgur or lentils with steamed asparagus or green beans on the side.

4 boneless chicken breasts
2 tablespoons yogurt
1/2 teaspoon salt
1/2 teaspoon mustard powder
2 teaspoons lemon juice
1/2 teaspoon curry powder

1 onion, quartered
4 tomatoes, sliced, for garnish
1 green pepper, sliced in rings, for garnish
few sprigs fresh mint or parsley, for garnish

Cut each chicken breast into 8 pieces.

Using the steel blade of a food processor or blender, blend yogurt, salt, mustard, lemon juice, curry and onion. Combine marinade with chicken. Cover and let stand 1 hour.

Broil chicken (or stir-saute in a skillet) until tender and cooked, about 20 minutes.

Transfer to a hot platter, or to individual serving plates. Garnish with tomatoes, green pepper rings and fresh mint or parsley.

MARINATED CHICKEN WITH OREGANO

Serves 8   *Bake at 425*

Serve with a baked potato, steamed cauliflower and carrots. Finish off the meal with a fruit cobbler!

4 pounds cut-up chicken
1/4 cup olive oil
1/4 cup lemon juice
1 teaspoon salt
1 tablespoon oregano

4 cloves garlic mashed with
   garlic press
1 teaspoon black pepper
a few sprigs watercress or
   parsley, for garnish

Place chicken, olive oil, lemon juice, salt, oregano, garlic and black pepper in a large bowl. Mix so chicken is well coated. Refrigerate, covered, for 24 hours.

Preheat grill. Remove chicken from marinade and grill, skin side down. Cook over the lowest heat with the cover down. Turn after 15 minutes and baste with remaining marinade. Grill for another 10-15 minutes.

Marinated chicken may also be baked in a hot, 425-degree oven for 30-45 minutes.

Garnish with a sprig of watercress or parsley.

CHICKEN WITH 40 CLOVES OF GARLIC

Serves 10   *Bake at 325*

The aroma of garlic permeates the house and makes mouths water. Baked garlic cloves can be pressed, and the garlic, which is buttery and mild, used on bread or potatoes.

5 chicken thighs	2 stalks celery, sliced
5 chicken breast halves	1 teaspoon thyme
40 cloves garlic, unpeeled	1 teaspoon rosemary
and left whole	1 teaspoon tarragon
2 carrots, sliced	1 teaspoon salt
2 kohlrabi, diced	1 teaspoon black pepper
	parsley sprigs, for garnish

Wash and pat chicken dry. Broil until the skin is crisp and brown, about 10 minutes.

Preheat oven to 325 degrees. Place chicken in a roasting pan together with unpeeled garlic cloves, carrots, kohlrabi, celery and herbs. Cover pan with foil, then place a lid over foil. Bake chicken 1-1/2 hours. Uncover during the last 15 minutes. Chicken is done when fork inserted into thigh comes out easily and juice runs clear.

Transfer chicken to a platter. Using slotted spoon, remove cloves of garlic and scatter around platter. Spoon vegetables over chicken. Sprinkle with salt and pepper, if desired.

Serve at once with crusty bread, baked potatoes and a green salad.

ARTICHOKE, CHICKPEA AND FENNEL GIAMBOTTA

Serves 8

An Italian stew which incorporates a unique blend of herbs, chicken, artichoke hearts, and chickpeas. Have fun with this recipe. To make it vegetarian, add firm tofu (2 pounds) instead of chicken. Or add cubes of potatoes or sweet potatoes instead of the chicken.

8 chicken thighs or breasts
2 teaspoons dried basil
2 teaspoons dried parsley
4 cloves garlic, minced
3 plum tomatoes
2 red bell-peppers, chopped coarsely
1 large zucchini, halved, sliced in 1-inch pieces
1 fennel bulb, halved, sliced, or 1 teaspoon dried fennel seed

1/2 teaspoon each thyme, oregano, black and red pepper
2 bay leaves
1-1/2 teaspoons salt
4 cups cooked, drained chickpeas or use other beans such as lima
2 tablespoons olive oil
1 teaspoon wine vinegar
8 artichoke hearts

Broil chicken until crisp and brown, about 15-20 minutes. Set aside while preparing the remainder of the dish.

Place herbs, chopped garlic and diced tomatoes in a large flame-proof casserole or kettle. Add red pepper and fennel. Mix in chickpeas together with 1 cup of their stock, olive oil, wine vinegar, and artichoke hearts. Bring to a boil. Add chicken, cover, and simmer over low heat for 15-20 minutes, or until the chicken is tender.

Remove bay leaves and stir in zucchini. Serve to oohs and aahs.

This stew also works beautifully with a firm white fish such as haddock. Simply add fish to stew during the last 10 minutes.

CHICKEN AND SHRIMP JAMBALAYA

Serves 4

From steamy New Orleans comes this lively and aromatic dish. Bring on the jazz band!

2 tablespoons olive oil
4 ribs celery, sliced
1 large onion, chopped
4 cloves garlic, minced
1 green pepper, chopped
1 6-ounce package Fakin' Bacon, chopped
2 cups boneless chicken, cut in bite-sized pieces
1 cup raw short-grain brown rice

2 cups tomatoes, chopped, liquid drained
1 8-ounce bottle clam juice
1 cup water
1/2 teaspoon thyme
3 bay leaves
1/2 pound shrimp, shelled and deveined
1 bunch scallions
salt and pepper to taste

Gently warm olive oil in a large skillet and saute celery, onion, garlic and pepper together with Fakin' Bacon and chicken until vegetables are tender and bacon is nicely browned. Add rice and stir one minute. Add tomatoes and their liquid, together with clam juice, water, bay leaves and thyme.

Simmer, covered until rice has cooked, about 45 minutes. Add shrimp and cook until they turn pink, about 3-4 minutes. Add chopped green onions and stir in gently.

Taste, adjust seasonings and serve hot!

CALZONES WITH POTATO AND TURKEY SAUSAGE

Serves 6   *Bake at 450*

One of our favorite calzone fillings.

Dough
1-1/2 teaspoons baking yeast	**1/4 cup olive oil**
1 cup lukewarm water	☐
1 teaspoon honey	**3 cups whole wheat flour**
☐	**1 teaspoon salt**

Sprinkle yeast over warm water and honey. Stir to dissolve. Let mixture stand 5 minutes, or until yeast is foamy. Stir in olive oil.

Whirl flour and salt together using the steel blade of a food processor. With machine running, pour yeast mixture through feed tube.

Process until dough is smooth and cleans the sides of the workbowl, about 30 seconds. Add more water (a teaspoonful at a time) if dough will not form a ball, or more flour if dough seems sticky. (Dough will be somewhat sticky until after first rise.) "Knead" 15-20 seconds. Place dough in a bowl. Cover with plastic wrap or a shower cap and let rise until doubled in bulk, about 30 minutes.

Prepare filling while dough rises.

Filling
4 large potatoes, cubed	**6 cloves garlic, finely minced**
6 tablespoons olive oil	**1 teaspoon black pepper**
2 large onions, finely chopped	**6 ounces turkey sausage**

Cook potatoes until soft, 10-15 minutes, in a small pot, using just enough water to cover them. Drain and mash with a potato masher or a wooden spoon.

Gently warm olive oil in a skillet. Saute onions and garlic until onion is transparent, about 5 minutes. Add mixture to potatoes together with black pepper.

Slice turkey sausage in 1/4 inch rounds.

Final Preparation

Preheat oven to 450 degrees.

Punch down risen dough. Divide into 6 pieces and using a rolling pin, roll out in rounds 1/4-inch thick. Place 1/6 potato filling onto one end of each calzone, divide turkey sausage and place atop potato filling. Fold empty side over and pinch edges together to seal filling. Prick calzone so steam can escape.

Bake on an oiled tray for 15-20 minutes, or until crisp and lightly browned.

Instead of turkey sausage, add 1/2 cup pine nuts, 1 cup raisins and 1 teaspoon allspice to potato filling. Or mash 2 cups pesto into potato.

CHICKEN CREOLE

Serves 8

Creole cooking -- robust, animated by the trinity of onions, celery and green peppers. Serve over artichoke noodles or rice.

8 assorted chicken pieces (i.e., thighs and breasts)
1/4 cup olive oil
2 large onions, chopped
4 cloves garlic, minced
2 ribs celery, sliced
2 green peppers, chopped coarsely
2 cups diced tomatoes
1 lemon, thinly sliced
1/4 teaspoon cayenne pepper
1/4 teaspoon black pepper
1 teaspoon salt
1 teaspoon chili powder
1 teaspoon basil
1/2 teaspoon thyme
4 bay leaves
2 bunches scallions, sliced
2 sprigs parsley

Broil chicken until crisp and brown, about 15-20 minutes. Remove and set aside.

Gently warm olive oil in a heavy Dutch oven or large skillet. Saute onions, garlic, celery and pepper slowly until vegetables begin to change color and become transparent, about 5 minutes. Add tomatoes and cook for another 5 minutes.

Add lemon, cayenne, black pepper, salt, basil, thyme, chili powder and bay leaves. Simmer 15 minutes. Add water if needed. Add chicken to creole mixture and cook 30 minutes, or until chicken is tender.

Remove dish from the stove. Taste and correct seasoning. Garnish with scallions and parsley. Serve with noodles or rice.

PERSIAN STUFFED EGGPLANT

Serves 8   *Bake at 375*

A distinctive dish with a flavorful stuffing, which may also be used to stuff zucchini, peppers, or tomatoes, or as an accompaniment to beans.

4 medium eggplants

1/3 cup yellow split peas
1-1/2 cups water

2 tablespoons olive oil
1 onion, minced
1 pound ground turkey

1/2 cup walnuts, chopped
1/2 cup raisins
1/2 teaspoon dried coriander
1/2 teaspoon dried ginger
salt and black pepper to taste

wedges of lemon and sprigs of
parsley for garnish

Cut eggplants in half the long way, leaving stem intact. Place cut side down on an oiled baking sheet. Cover and bake at 375 degrees until tender, about 30-40 minutes.

While eggplant is baking, cover split peas with several inches water in a small pot and cook for 30 minutes, or until they just begin to disintegrate. Drain cooked split peas and set aside.

Gently warm olive oil in a skillet and saute onions until soft, about 5 minutes. Add ground turkey and stir until no pink remains. Add nuts, raisins, coriander and ginger. Add split peas and stir. Season to taste with salt and pepper.

Turn baked eggplant halves over in baking pan. With a fork or spoon mash pulp, taking care not to break the skin. Push aside pulp, making a hollow in each half. Divide filling between eggplants and bake another 15 minutes, until browned on top.

Serve with a wedge of lemon and a sprig of parley.

Seafood Main Dishes

SEAFOOD

We love seafood because it is "heart-healthy" and delicious. Seafood can be combined with everything from saffron to basil to artichoke hearts and chickpeas.

When buying fresh fish, look for fish with eyes that are clear and not sunken. The body should be firm and bounce back when poked. There should be only a mild odor, or none at all. If a fish smells fishy, then it's not fresh. Remember, when storing fresh fish in the refrigerator, wrap loosely and use within a day. Store frozen fish in its original wrapping in the freezer where it will last a considerable time.

Like poultry, rinse seafood before using.

Fish is done when fillets can be flaked easily with a fork.

SHRIMP AND FISH CASSEROLE WITH ROMANO

Serves 6

Three favorite foods, shrimp, fish and Pecorino Romano cheese give this dish a festive air. Serve over pasta or rice.

2 tablespoons olive oil
1 onion, chopped
3 cloves garlic, minced
☐
1 15-ounce can tomatoes
3/4 teaspoon oregano
1 teaspoon black pepper
☐

2 pounds cod, scrod, haddock,
    or halibut, in 3/4 inch pieces
1/4 pound medium raw shrimp,
    peeled and deveined
☐
3/4 cup grated Pecorino
    Romano cheese
parsley for garnish

Gently warm olive oil in a large skillet. Saute onion and garlic until soft, about 5 minutes.

Stir in tomatoes, oregano and pepper. Bring to a boil. Reduce heat, cover and simmer 10 minutes, stirring occasionally.

Add fish to skillet and stir to coat. Cover and simmer 10 minutes. Add shrimp and cook, uncovered, just until shrimp turn pink, about 5 minutes.

Serve at once over pasta and sprinkle with Romano. Garnish with parsley.

SHRIMP CURRY WITH POTATOES

Serves 8

Accompany with steamed asparagus or spinach. Or, make with 2 pounds tofu instead of shrimp. In this case, you may want to increase the amount of spices.

8 medium red potatoes, scrubbed, unpeeled and cut into quarters
□
4 tablespoons olive oil
4 onions, chopped
1 teaspoon salt
1 teaspoon ground coriander

1 teaspoon curry
1 1-pound can Italian peeled tomatoes, drained
2 pounds peeled and deveined shrimp
□
1 lemon
watercress for garnish

Steam or bake potatoes until tender when pierced by a fork. Set aside.

Gently warm olive oil in a skillet. Saute onions until tender, about 5 minutes. Add spices and stir over low heat 5 minutes. Add tomatoes, shrimp and cooked potatoes. Simmer just until tomatoes are hot and shrimp have turned pink, another 5 minutes. Squeeze juice of lemon over entire dish.

Garnish with watercress and serve at once.

CAJUN SHRIMP JAMBALAYA

Serves 8

Shrimp with a Louisiana beat. Yumm!

1/4 cup olive oil	1 teaspoon thyme
2 onions, chopped	1/2 teaspoon cayenne pepper
4 cloves garlic, minced	1 teaspoon black pepper
1 teaspoon hot pepper flakes	2 cups raw Basmati rice
1 6-oz. package Fakin' Bacon	☐
2 green peppers, diced	1/4 cup dried parsley
☐	☐
3 cups diced tomatoes	salt to taste
☐	☐
3 cups water	2 pounds large shrimp

Gently warm olive oil in a skillet. Saute onions and garlic together with hot pepper flakes, Fakin' Bacon and peppers until onions are soft, about 5 minutes. Add tomatoes and simmer 10 minutes, stirring occasionally.

Add water, thyme, cayenne, black pepper and rice to skillet. Bring jambalaya to a boil. Cover and simmer 40 minutes, or until rice is tender. Stir in parsley. Taste and adjust seasoning.

Add shrimp to skillet, cover and cook 3-5 minutes, until shrimp turn pink.

THAI-SCENTED SHRIMP KEBABS

Serves 6-8

The key to making delicious kebabs is in the long marination. So marinate this the night before.

14 ounces unsweetened
  coconut milk
1/2 cup lemon or lime juice
2 tablespoons minced ginger
2 cloves garlic, minced
3 tablespoons soy sauce
1 tablespoon rice syrup
1 teaspoon dried lemon grass
1 tablespoon sesame or olive oil
1/2 teaspoon salt
1/2 teaspoon crushed red
  pepper

2 pounds large shrimp, peeled
  and deveined
2 red bell peppers, cut
  into 24 triangles
□
1 tablespoon black sesame
  seeds
1/2 cup chopped parsley

In a small pan, whisk coconut milk with lemon or lime juice, ginger, garlic, soy sauce, rice syrup, lemon grass, oil, salt and crushed red pepper. Bring to a boil over moderately high heat and boil 1 minute. Set aside to cool.

Pour cooled marinade over shrimp. Refrigerate covered, for at least 12 hours and up to 24.

Preheat a broiler. Mix shrimp with peppers and broil in marinade, turning once, until shrimp are cooked through and the peppers charred, about 5 minutes. Transfer to a platter and sprinkle with sesame seeds and chopped parsley.

Serve with black or red Thai rice.

SCALLOP SAUTE WITH CHINESE VEGETABLES

Serves 8-10

Savory and slightly sweet, garnish with toasted soynuts or cashews.

2 pounds scallops
1/4 cup tamari soy sauce
1/4 cup olive or sesame oil
4 cloves garlic, minced
1 teaspoon black pepper
   □
1 cup toasted soynuts or
   cashews for garnish

2 4-oz. cans sliced water
   chestnuts
2 4-oz. cans bamboo shoots
1 pound snow peas, stringed
a handful of dulse (mild tasting,
   salty seaweed)
2 cups mushrooms, thickly
   sliced

Marinate scallops for two hours, or up to 24, in tamari, oil, garlic and black pepper.

If using cashews, toast on a cookie sheet in a 250 degree oven for 15 minutes. Set aside to cool.

Heat a wok or large skillet and stir-fry scallops in marinade until opaque, about 3 minutes. Add vegetables and stir-fry just until snow peas have turned bright green and dulse has turned red, about 2 minutes.

Serve immediately over rice noodles or hot rice. Garnish with soynuts or cashews.

RUSSIAN FISH CAKES

Serves 6

Succulent fish cakes with a crispy coating. Accompany with cucumber rounds or coleslaw. Garnish with a sprig of fresh dill.

2 tablespoons olive oil	**1 tablespoon black pepper**
2 onions, finely chopped	**salt to taste**
□	□
3 slices wholegrain bread	**1/4 cup plain no-fat yogurt**
□	**1/4 cup mayonnaise or**
1-1/2 pound haddock, cod, or	**Nayonaise**
halibut cut into 2-inch pieces	**1 teaspoon dried dill weed**
1 large carrot, grated	□
1 teaspoon dried dill weed	**3 tablespoons olive oil**
3 tablespoons lemon juice	**1 cup soy granules or grits**
	sprigs of dill to garnish

Gently warm olive oil in a medium skillet. Add onions and saute until golden, 10 minutes. Transfer to a large bowl.

Using the steel blade of a food processor, process bread in food processor into crumbs. Process fish with on/off turns until ground, but not pureed. Transfer to bowl. Use the grating disk to grate carrot or grate by hand. Add carrot together with dill, lemon and pepper to fish. Knead well to blend. Cover and refrigerate 1 hour to firm fish.

Mix yogurt, mayonnaise or Nayonaise and dill. Set aside.

Form fish into 3-inch oval patties. Heat oil in a large, heavy skillet. Coat patties in soy granules. Saute fish cakes over medium heat until golden, about 4 minutes per side. Serve with a dollop of yogurt sauce and garnish with a sprig of dill.

MEDITERRANEAN FISH STEW

Serves 4

A classic fish stew with a wonderful blend of basil, oregano, tomato, lemon and saffron. Serve with crusty brown bread or over rice.

1/4 cup olive oil	2 cups diced tomatoes
1 large onion, chopped	2 tablespoons lemon juice or
5 cloves garlic, minced	vinegar
□	□
1 tablespoon dried parsley	1-1/2 pounds cod or haddock,
1 teaspoon basil	cut into chunks
1 teaspoon oregano	1/2 pound scallops
1 teaspoon black pepper	1 cup minced clams with liquid
1/2 teaspoon turmeric	□
pinch saffron	salt to taste

Gently warm olive oil in a large skillet. Add onion and garlic and saute until onion is soft, about 5 minutes. Stir in parsley, basil, oregano, black pepper, turmeric and a pinch of saffron. Add tomatoes and lemon or vinegar and simmer 5 minutes.

Stir in fish, scallops, and clams with liquid and simmer until fish is tender, about 20 minutes.

Taste and add salt if desired.

FISH BAKED WITH PESTO

Serves 6-8   *Bake at 450*

Rich, creamy pesto without nuts accompanies fresh fish. Serve with a grain pilaf and garnish with a sprig of parsley or watercress.

4 scallions, in 1-inch pieces
4 large cloves garlic
1/2 packed cup fresh parsley
1/4 cup fresh basil or tarragon
** leaves**
1-1/2 teaspoons lemon peel

2 tablespoons olive oil
1 teaspoon black pepper
salt to taste
3-4 pounds fish fillets (a firm
** white fish of your choice)**

Preheat oven to 450 degrees.

Using the steel blade of a food processor, blend scallions, garlic, parsley, basil or tarragon, lemon peel, olive oil and black pepper. Stop the machine once or twice to scrape down the sides of the workbowl. Taste pesto and season with salt if desired.

Arrange fish fillets in a baking dish and spread with pesto. Turn fish over and coat second side. Bake uncovered, until tender, about 20 minutes.

GREEK FISH SPETSIOTIKO

Serves 6-8   *Bake at 350*

Fish stew with a mix of tomatoes, olives, garlic and oregano. Typically Greek, typically delicious.

3-4 pounds thick white fish fillets	**1 teaspoon black pepper**
□	**6 cloves garlic, minced**
2 tablespoons olive oil	□
3 large onions, sliced	**4 hot boiled potatoes, diced**
2 cups diced tomatoes	**3 tablespoons lemon juice**
1/4 cup coarsely chopped olives	**salt to taste**
1 teaspoon oregano	

Preheat oven to 350 degrees.

Gently warm olive oil in a skillet. Saute onion until translucent, about 5 minutes. Add tomatoes, olives, oregano, pepper and garlic. Cover and simmer sauce 5 minutes to give the flavors a chance to blend.

Arrange fish in a baking dish. Add diced potatoes and sauce. Stir and bake, uncovered, until fish flakes easily, about 30 minutes.

When stew is removed from oven, squeeze lemon juice over fish. Taste and adjust seasoning.

HERBED SALMON SAUTEED WITH VEGETABLES

Serves 4

Tender, rosy, juicy salmon steaks with vegetables beneath. Serve with wild or wehani rice.

2 cups water
1 cup wild or wehani rice
□
4 salmon steaks
□
2 carrots, grated
1 stalk celery, sliced
1 large zucchini, sliced
1 large onion, chopped

1 medium tomato, diced
pinch basil, oregano, thyme
    and marjoram
4 teaspoons lemon juice
2 teaspoons olive oil
1 teaspoon black pepper
□
lemon wedges for garnish

Bring water to a boil. Stir in rice, cover pot, lower heat and simmer 45 minutes. After 45 minutes, turn off heat and let rice sit in pot, covered, while preparing dish.

Mix vegetables with herbs. Place in a large frying pan or skillet with a cover. Arrange salmon steaks over vegetables. Mix lemon juice and olive oil and pour over fish. Sprinkle with black pepper. Cover pan and simmer 10 minutes.

To serve, place some rice on one-third of the plate, then salmon to the side, garnished with lemon wedges, and vegetables on the remaining third. Salt lightly, if desired.

This yields a light and tender fish and is also suitable for "refreshing" frozen salmon, which might otherwise cook up dry.

HERBED HADDOCK STEW WITH POTATOES

Serves 4

The herbs make a simple stew fragrant and lovely. For a refreshing dessert, serve strawberries with raspberry sauce.

1/4 cup olive oil
2 large onions, chopped
1 clove garlic, minced
1 tomato, diced or 1/4 cup
  tomato sauce
1 green pepper, diced
2 stalks celery, sliced
  ☐
2 bay leaves

1/4 teaspoon each cayenne,
  oregano, basil, thyme
1/2 cup water
4 potatoes, cubed
  ☐
2 pounds haddock fillets, cut
  1-inch thick
  ☐
salt to taste, if desired

Gently warm olive oil in a skillet and saute vegetables. Add herbs, spices, water and cubed potatoes. Cover and simmer 10 minutes, or until mixture is soft and slightly brown.

Place fish on top. Cover and simmer 10 minutes, turn fish and cook another 10. Taste and adjust seasoning.

To serve, place haddock on the side of the plate with the stew beside it.

Substitute halibut, cod, red snapper, or any favorite fish fillet or steak.

MARINATED SOLE WITH PINE NUTS

Serves 6

The delicate flavor and texture of sole combines with wine and the lusciousness of pine nuts.

2 tablespoons olive oil	**☐**
4 onions, halved and sliced	**2 tablespoons olive oil**
☐	**2 pounds sole fillets**
1/2 cup dry white wine or	**☐**
** lemon juice**	**1/2 cup dry white wine**
1/2 cup cider vinegar	**1/2 cup cider vinegar**
1/4 cup pine nuts	

Gently warm 2 tablespoons olive oil in a skillet. Saute onions until tender, stirring occasionally, about 5 minutes. Stir in wine, vinegar, and pine nuts. Set aside.

Heat 2 tablespoons olive oil in another skillet. Add sole and saute over medium heat until opaque, 2 minutes per side. Carefully cut sole into bite-sized pieces. Transfer fish to a glass or ceramic pan. Pour the remaining 1/2 cup wine and vinegar over fish. Spoon onion mixture over as well.

Cover and refrigerate 2 days to let the flavors blend.

Bring to room temperature before serving.

SOLE WITH BUTTER AND ALMONDS

Serves 4

Deliciously decadent - almonds browned in butter spooned over sole. Equally luscious and rich olive oil can be used in place of butter.

4 sole fillets, about 1-1/2 pounds	**1/4 cup dry white wine**
□	**2 tablespoons fresh lemon juice**
6 tablespoons butter	□
1/2 cup almonds	**lemon wedges, for garnish**

Melt butter in a large skillet over medium high heat. Add almonds and cook until heated through, about 1 minute.

Add wine and lemon juice to skillet. Simmer until sauce is slightly thickened, stirring constantly.

Broil sole 2 minutes. Turn and pour sauce over fish and broil for another 2 minutes.

Serve garnished with lemon wedges. Accompany with boiled rice.

COLD POACHED FISH WITH AIOLI

Serves 6

An ideal party dish on a warm summer night.

**2 pounds leftover firm, baked
  or broiled fish, such as
  haddock or tuna**
  □
**1/4 cup fresh lemon juice
1 egg yolk
2 large cloves garlic**

**1/4 teaspoon dried mustard
pinch cayenne pepper
1/2 teaspoon salt
3/4 cup olive or sesame oil
2 tablespoons plain non-fat
  yogurt**

This dish assumes one has had the foresight to cook fish ahead. If not, bake or broil fish until translucent and flesh parts easily with a fork.

Using a food processor or blender, blend lemon juice, egg yolk, garlic cloves, mustard, cayenne pepper and salt. With the machine running, slowly pour oil through feed tube. Mix in yogurt.

Aioli is also great on cold vegetables and potatoes.

Desserts

DESSERTS

Fresh fruit is the simplest and most perfect dessert. But, when you're ready to "sin", do it in style. Do it the old-fashioned way by using the best of everything - the freshest nuts and the best cream, one without preservatives.

Honey, which we use frequenly as a sweetener, is also a healer. Germs won't grow in honey, and when applied to a cut or burn, it works magic.

Should your honey crystallize, set the jar in a bowl of hot water until the crystals have dissolved.

We also use rice syrup and barley malt. Not as sweet as honey, they metabolize more slowly and may be eaten by those who cannot handle faster acting sugars. Date sugar made from dried pulverized dates, and stevia, a South American herb many times sweeter than sucrose, are other natural sweeteners available on the market.

Many of the candies, cakes, cookies, and other pastries that follow are special occasion treats. But, dessert can be healthy too! Check out Fruit Compote with Berries (p. 307), Strawberries with Raspberry Sauce (p. 308), Apple Brown Betty (p. 309), Plum and Blueberry Crisp (p. 310), Apricot Fluff (p. 311), Rhubarb with Barley (p. 312), and Apple-Cranberry Streusel Pie (p. 313). Here the emphasis is on fruit and whole grains rather than sugar and fat.

SESAME SPICE CANDY

Makes 48

Old-world candies redolent with cinnamon and ginger.

Don't make on a rainy day as honey absorbs moisture and candies will be sticky. If sticky, candy may be frozen until ready to eat.

2 cups brown sesame seeds	**1/2 cup barley malt**
□	**1/2 teaspoon cinnamon**
1/4 cup honey	**1/4 teaspoon ginger**

Grease a 12x12 shallow baking pan.

Toast sesame seeds in an ungreased skillet, stirring over medium-high heat 5-10 minutes until aromatic and seeds begin to pop. Transfer to a bowl, making sure that there are no seeds left in the skillet.

Put honey, barley malt, cinnamon and ginger in skillet and bring to a full rolling boil over low heat, stirring often. Cook syrup 4 minutes. Remove skillet from heat and quickly stir in sesame seeds. Quickly turn hot mixture into prepared pan. Using a light touch, pat out with rubber spatula and then the palm of your hand. A heavy touch will cause hot candy to stick. If necessary, wet hands with cold water to pat. Do this sparingly, so honey won't have much water to absorb.

Cool candy 10 minutes, then test to see if cool enough to cut into squares and squares into triangles. Don't wait too long to cut or candy will harden. Once cut, cool completely before storing in an airtight container.

BIRDSEED CLUSTERS

Makes 16

Similar to sesame spice candies, birdseed clusters have a different charm and are, perhaps, easier to make because they don't have to be cut or patted out.

1 cup sunflower seeds	**1/2 cup barley malt**
1 cup pumpkin seeds	**1/2 teaspoon cinnamon**
☐	**1/4 teaspoon ginger**
1/4 cup honey	

Grease two 12x12 shallow baking pans or cookie sheets.

Follow the directions for making Sesame Spice Candy.

Instead of spooning batter into prepared pans and patting out, use a 1/4 cup measure or large soup spoon and dollop out clumps of hot mixture onto pans. When batter is distributed, use the heel of your hand to flatten clusters. Don't press too hard as candy may still be hot and can burn.

Cool 10 minutes and then remove clusters with a metal spatula. Place on serving plate in a single layer so candies don't "melt" into one another.

Candies may be frozen on cookie sheets for a few minutes before removing with a metal spatula. Then stack and store in the freezer. When frozen, candies are brittle, so don't drop!

CAROB CONFECTIONS

Makes approx 42 balls

No-bake, fudge-like confections. Glossy and chocolaty.

1 cup honey	1 cup sesame seeds
1 cup unsalted, crunchy	1/2 cup wheat germ
peanut butter	1/2 cup soy granules
☐	1 teaspoon cinnamon
1 cup carob powder	1 teaspoon almond extract
1 cup sunflower seeds	

Beat honey and peanut butter together until "liquidy," using a wooden spoon.

Only then, mix in dry ingredients and extract. Again, use a wooden spoon or knead with your hands. Dough will be sticky, stiff and hard to mix. Persevere!

Pinch off pieces of dough about the size of walnuts and roll between your hands until smooth and shiny.

Store confections in the refrigerator, but bring to room temperature before eating.

SESAME TREATS

Makes 24

Make an extra batch to tuck into lunchboxes or to have on hand for the midnight nibbler.

1/4 cup desiccated coconut	1/2 cup tahini
3/4 cup sunflower seeds	1/2 cup honey
1/2 cup wheat germ	1/2 teaspoon cinnamon
1/2 cup bran	1 teaspoon almond extract

Blend all the ingredients together using the steel blade of a food processor and on/off turns until sunflower seeds are finely ground.

Divide mixture in half; form into two rolls 1-inch in diameter. Wrap rolls in waxed paper and store in refrigerator. Slice to serve.

Candy may also be pressed into a large baking pan. Cut into squares to serve.

MAPLE ALMOND CHEWS

Makes 24 bars   *Bake at 300*

Kids love to make these.

1 cup almonds   **1/2 cup carob chips**
☐   ☐
1 cup puffed cereal   **1/2 cup maple syrup**

Preheat oven to 300 degrees.

Roast almonds on a cookie sheet for 15 minutes. Remove from the oven and set aside to cool completely.

Coarsely chop almonds using the steel blade of a food processor and on/off turns. Remove nuts to a mixing bowl. Add puffed cereal and carob chips. Mix and set aside.

Grease an 8-inch square pan.

Bring maple syrup to a boil. Pour over dry ingredients and stir quickly. Press batter into cookie pan.

Chill maple almond chews in the refrigerator 2 hours. Cut into squares and serve.

Best eaten the day they are made.

Try substituting granola for puffed cereal.

ORANGE SEED STRIPS

Makes 18 large cookies   *Bake at 300*

My version of a favorite from Brownies Restaurant in New York City, an institution which is, sadly, no more.

1/4 cup powdered milk	2 teaspoons vanilla
2-1/2 cups w/w pastry flour	1 teaspoon orange extract
1/2 cup soy flour	1 tablespoon water
1/2 teaspoon cinnamon	□
1 cup raw sugar or Sucanat	1/2 cup sunflower seeds
1/2 cup safflower oil	1/2 cup brown sesame seeds
2 eggs (reserve 1 white)	sesame seeds for sprinkling

Preheat oven to 300 degrees.   Grease two cookie sheets.

Mix all ingredients except sunflower and sesame seeds using the steel blade of a food processor and on/off turns until the batter moves freely under the blade. Knead dough by running machine for another minute, stopping once or twice to scrape down sides of the workbowl with a rubber spatula.

Add sunflower and sesame seeds.   Quickly turn machine on/off several times to incorporate seeds.

Divide dough into 4 balls and roll each into a 9-inch rope. Place on cookie sheets and flatten 4 inches wide.   Brush each with reserved egg white mixed with 1-2 tablespoons water. Sprinkle cookies with sesame seeds.

Bake 30 minutes, or until nicely browned and aromatic. Remove from oven and cut into 2-inch strips.

CHEWY BAR COOKIES

Makes 24   *Bake at 350*

Moist and chewy. Easy to make.

3 eggs
1 cup maple syrup
1 cup unsweetened shredded
    coconut
1 cup raisins, or date
    pieces in oat flour

3/4 cup w/w pastry flour
1/4 cup wheat germ
1 teaspoon cinnamon
1 teaspoon vanilla
1 cup chopped walnuts
1 cup carob chips

Preheat oven to 350 degrees.

Grease a 9-inch square baking pan.

Mix the ingredients together and spread batter evenly in pan. Bake 20 minutes, or until cookies are slightly brown around the edges and a toothpick inserted in the center comes out clean.

When cookies are done, remove pan from oven and cool slightly before cutting into squares or bars.

WALNUT SURPRISE COOKIES

Makes 16 squares   *Bake at 350*

Walnut surprise cookies have sentimental value - the first cookie my brothers and I learned to make. Impossible to eat just one!

1 cup turbinado sugar or Sucanat	*1/2 cup w/w pastry flour*
1 egg	*1/4 teaspoon salt*
1 teaspoon vanilla	*1 cup walnuts, chopped*
□	*1/2 cup carob chips*

Preheat oven to 350 degrees. Grease an 8-inch square cookie pan.

Beat together with a wooden spoon until "liquidy" the sugar, eggs and vanilla. Mix in flour and salt. Add walnuts and mix well. At this point the batter will be thick and sticky and hard to mix.

Spread batter in pan. Start by pushing batter into corners with the wooden spoon and finish by patting into an even layer with your fingers and the palm of the hand.

Bake cookies 20 minutes, or until lightly brown and edges of the batter pull away from the sides of the pan.

Remove from oven and place pan on cooling rack for 10 minutes. While cookies are still warm, cut into large squares.

To "frost," sprinkle carob chips on top as soon as cookies come out of the oven. The heat will soften the chips, and they can be spread with a butter knife and light touch.

TAHINI KEENIES

Makes 36 cookies   *Bake at 350*

Tahini, or sesame butter, rich in calcium and minerals, is an excellent source of protein. Tahini Keenies are a meal in themselves.

1-1/2 cups tahini   **2 teaspoons cinnamon**
2 cups honey   **6-8 cups rolled oats**

Beat together tahini and honey in a large bowl with a heavy wooden spoon until "liquidy" and creamy. Blend in cinnamon and oats. (This mixture will be quite sticky!)

Grease cookie sheets and preheat oven to 350 degrees.

Drop dough by tablespoonfuls onto cookie sheets. Flatten slightly with palm of hands. If batter sticks to your hands, wet them.

Bake cookies for 20-25 minutes, or until lightly golden. Place cookie sheet on wire racks to cool for 5-10 minutes. When cool, remove cookies with a metal spatula to cool completely on racks.

PEANUT BUTTER CAROB CHIP COOKIES

Makes 36 large cookies   *Bake at 350*

Very like tahini keenies. Here, peanut butter and carob chips combine in a satisfying treat.

1-1/2 cups peanut butter   *6-8 cups rolled oats*
2 cups honey   □
□   *1 cup raisins*
2 teaspoons cinnamon   *2 cups carob chips*

Preheat oven to 350 degrees. Grease cookie sheets.

Beat together peanut butter and honey in a mixing bowl using a wooden spoon until "liquidy."

Blend cinnamon with oatmeal and add to cookie batter. Still using the wooden spoon, mix in oats. Batter will become difficult to mix because it will be thick and sticky. Mix in raisins and carob chips.

Drop batter by tablespoonful onto cookie sheets and flatten slightly with hands.

Bake cookies 10-15 minutes. When golden brown, take cookie sheets out of oven and place on racks to cool 10 minutes. Remove cookies from sheets with metal spatula and finish cooling on racks.

Store in cookie jar or freezer.

WALNUT CAROB BROWNIES

Makes 24 cookies   *Bake at 350*

Carob, with the look of chocolate, has its own taste appeal.

1/2 cup carob powder
1/2 cup w/w pastry flour
1/4 teaspoon cinnamon
1/2 teaspoon salt
1 teaspoon baking powder
        □
2 eggs

2/3 cup canola or safflower oil
1 teaspoon vanilla extract
1/4 cup honey
1/4 cup barley malt
        □
1 cup walnuts

Preheat oven to 350 degrees. Grease an 8-inch square cookie pan.

Blend dry ingredients, except for walnuts, using the steel blade of a food processor. Add wet ingredients and whirl for a few seconds, stopping the machine once or twice to scrape down the sides of the workbowl with a rubber spatula. (Alternatively, the dry ingredients can be mixed together in a bowl, the wet mixed in another bowl, and the two added together. Walnuts can be chopped by hand to stir in.)

Add walnuts and chop in with several on/off turns. Spoon batter into pan and bake 30 minutes, or until cookies begin to pull away from the sides of the pan and a toothpick inserted in the center comes out clean.

Remove pan from the oven to place on a rack and cool cookies completely before cutting into squares.

OATMEAL RAISIN COOKIES

Makes 24 2-1/2 inch cookies   *Bake at 350*

This wonderful recipe comes from Kathleen Jordan, Allergy Alternatives, Concord, Massachusetts, and is wheat and egg-free.

2 teaspoons EnerG brand egg replacer
2 tablespoons water
1/2 cup honey
1/2 cup vegetable oil such as canola or safflower
1-1/2 cups rolled oats

1/2 cup raisins
1/2 cup dairy-free carob chips
1 cup spelt flour
1/2 teaspoon baking soda
1/4 teaspoon salt

Preheat oven to 350 degrees. Take out two cookie sheets, but do not grease.

In a large bowl, whisk together egg replacer and water. Add honey and oil and whisk until mixture is bubbly.

Add oats, raisins, and carob chips and stir to mix.

Sift together flour, soda, and salt. Add to wet mixture. Drop cookie batter by rounded teaspoonsfull onto ungreased cookie sheets. Bake 7-9 minutes, until lightly browned on edges.

Remove cookie sheets from oven to place on a rack for 15 minutes. Then remove cookies from sheets with metal spatula and cool completely on rack before serving.

SUZEN'S GRANOLA BARS

Makes 48

We all love it when Suzen mixes up granola bars. They pack a nutritional wallop!

4 cups rolled oats
1 cup wheat, rye or barley flakes
1 cup crispy brown rice cereal
   or puffed cereal
1 cup sunflower seeds
1/2 cup sesame seeds
1/2 cup wheat germ or bran
1 cup sliced almonds
3/4 cup vegetable oil (canola or
   safflower)
1-1/4 cups honey

1/4 cup molasses
1 teaspoon vanilla or
   almond extract
1/3 cup sesame tahini or
   peanut butter
1 cup dates, raisins, or
   carob chips
1/2 cup coconut flakes
   (optional)
1/4 cup non-instant milk
   powder (optional)

Mix dry ingredients in a large bowl. Add wet ingredients and mix both together using your hands.

Grease two 11x17 pans and spread granola mixture onto pans with wet hands. Pat firmly until even.

Bake at 350 degrees 25-30 minutes, or until lightly browned. Cool 20 minutes before cutting into 20-24 pieces. Once completely cool, remove granola bars to an airtight container. Store extras in the freezer or individually wrap for on-the-go snacks.

PERFECT CAROB FROSTING

Makes enough for a 3-layer cake

A luscious, chocolaty frosting which remains glossy.

**12 ounces barley-malt sweetened
carob bar, chips or disks**

**1 cup heavy cream
1 tablespoon vanilla**

Using the steel blade of a food processor, chop carob bar with on\off turns. If using carob chips or disks no chopping is necessary. Place them in the workbowl of the processor.

In a small pot, scald cream over moderate heat until bubbles appear around the edges.

With the food processor running, pour hot cream through feed tube in a steady stream. Add vanilla. Process until frosting is smooth.

Let frosting cool to thicken. Don't stir during cooling in order to achieve a thick, fudgy consistency.

POT DE CREME CAROB

Serves 6

A lovely and rich carob mousse. Even those who profess to hate carob have been known to lick the bowl.

3/4 pound malt-sweetened carob block in 1/2-inch pieces or carob disks or chips

2 cups heavy cream
6 egg yolks
1-1/2 teaspoons vanilla

Using the steel blade of a food processor, chop carob bar with on/off turns. If using chips or disks, no chopping is necessary. Place them in the workbowl of the processor.

Bring cream to a boil. With the processor motor running, slowly pour cream through feed tube. Whirl until smooth, about 30 seconds. Add egg yolks one at a time. Blend 10 seconds after each. Add vanilla.

Pour pot de creme carob into six pot de creme pots or pretty liqueur glasses. Cover each. Refrigerate for several hours or overnight before serving.

Serve plain or with a dollop of whipped cream. To speed up serving time, freeze for 2 hours. Soften slightly in refrigerator before serving.

Save egg whites in a glass jar in the refrigerator to use in meringues for Baked Alaska or macaroons.

LIGHT CAROB MOUSSE

Serves 12

This smooth, low-calorie mousse was created especially for my mother, Beatrice, who loves carob.

1-1/2 tablespoons unflavored gelatin	☐
	5 eggs, separated
1/3 cup water	1/2 cup honey
☐	1/4 teaspoon salt
9 tablespoons carob powder	3 teaspoons vanilla extract
2/3 cup boiling water	1/4 teaspoon cinnamon

In a small bowl, whisk together gelatin and water. Let stand for five minutes.

In another bowl, whisk carob powder in boiling water until there are no lumps. Add gelatin to carob and stir until gelatin is dissolved.

Using an electric mixer, beat yolks, adding honey gradually, until light and fluffy. Add salt, vanilla and cinnamon. Pour carob mixture into yolks and mix until blended.

Using a clean dry beater and another mixing bowl, beat egg whites until they peak but are still moist. Quickly fold carob mixture into egg whites with a wire whisk. Pour batter into a large decorative bowl or individual serving glasses. Cover with plastic wrap and refrigerate 8 hours, or overnight, so that mousse is firm and flavors have a chance to blend.

Serve with a dollop of whipped cream, chopped nuts, or sprinkle of coconut.

BAVARIAN WHIPPED CREAM

Serves 6

A snap to prepare! Elegant served in wine goblets. Substitute vanilla yogurt for whipping cream for a low-calorie version.

1 cup heavy whipping cream
2 tablespoons honey or fruit
concentrate
1 teaspoon vanilla extract

2 cups fresh berries, peaches apricots, pitted cherries or blueberries

Perfect berries or fruit for garnish

Using an electric mixer, whip cream until stiff peaks form. Gradually beat in honey and vanilla.

Fold fruit into whipped cream with a rubber spatula. Spoon into goblets or dessert bowls. Cover and chill thoroughly before serving. Garnish with perfect berries or slices of whole fruit.

PORTUGESE MAPLE FLAN

Serves 10   *Bake at 300*

A rich maple custard -- the ultimate creamy dessert.

1 cup maple syrup   **4 eggs, room temperature**
□   **1 teaspoon vanilla extract**
3 cups half-and-half

Preheat oven to 300 degrees. In a small saucepan, bring 3/4 cup maple syrup to a boil over moderate heat. Boil, stirring occasionally, for 10 minutes. Remove pan from stove and stir briefly so foam subsides. Pour into a 6-cup ring mold (or use an oven-proof dish); tilt quickly to evenly coat bottom of mold.

In the same saucepan, bring half-and-half to a boil over moderate heat, stirring to dissolve remaining syrup.

Meanwhile, beat eggs with an electric mixer until thick. Drizzle in remaining 1/4 cup maple syrup. With mixer still running, gradually pour hot cream into beaten eggs. Stir in vanilla. Strain through a mesh strainer or cheesecloth into mold. Place mold in a larger pan, and place pan in the oven. Add enough hot water to reach halfway up the mold.

Bake 1 hour, or longer (sometimes as much as another 45 minutes, depending upon mold, weather, etc.) until custard is set and a knife inserted in the center comes out clean. Remove mold from water bath and cool. Refrigerate 3 hours or overnight.

To serve, run knife around the edge and invert flan onto a serving plate with a lip so syrup will not run on floor! Hit bottom of pan smartly with palm of your hand. Flan should come out. If not, repeat procedure.

ECLAIRS

Makes 8   *Bake at 425, 375*

Elegant. Fill with pastry cream, ice cream, custard, or sweetened whipped cream. Drizzle hot carob frosting on top. Yumm....

1 cup water	**2/3 cup w/w pastry flour**
1/2 cup butter	☐
3 tablespoons honey	**5 eggs (reserve one to glaze)**

Preheat oven to 425 degrees.

Heat water, butter and honey in heavy saucepan over medium heat until butter melts and water bubbles. Remove pot from heat and add flour all at once. Beat vigorously with a wooden spoon until thoroughly blended. Return the pot to the heat and continue to stir until dough comes away from sides of the pot and leaves the spoon clean. Remove saucepan from the heat.

Place dough in workbowl of a food processor. Using the steel blade and quick on/off turns, knead dough for 20 seconds, and then add the 4 eggs, one at a time, running the machine 20 seconds after each. Run machine another minute. Dough will be smooth and shiny. Shape into 8 hot-dog shaped mounds and place 2 inches apart on an ungreased cookie sheet. Mix reserved egg with 1/2 teaspoon water and brush eclairs. Bake 20 minutes. Reduce oven temperature to 375 degrees and bake another 10 minutes, or until eclairs are golden brown. Test for doneness by removing a puff from the sheet with a spatula. If it does not fall, they are done.

Make a slit in the side of each puff and return to turned-off oven for 10 minutes. Then remove from oven and pull out soft dough from the center of each. When completely cool, fill.

FRENCH PASTRY CREAM

Makes 2-1/2 cups

French pastry cream holds its shape when cold. Use to fill eclairs or a nut-crust tart.

1/2 cup honey
6 egg yolks
□
1/2 cup w/w pastry flour

□
2 cups milk
□
1 tablespoon vanilla extract

In a saucepan, warm honey over low heat. Add egg yolks, one at a time, beating vigorously with a wooden spoon after each addition. Mixture will turn creamy yellow. Add flour all at once and continue to beat until mixture is free of lumps.

In a separate sauce pan, bring milk to a boil. Slowly add milk to egg mixture, stirring constantly with a wire whisk. Cook over low heat until custard begins to bubble, about 5 minutes. Continue to cook and stir for another two minutes, being careful that pastry cream does not boil.

Remove pot with thickened cream from heat and add extract. As the mixture cools, stir occasionally to prevent crust from forming.

Save egg whites in a glass jar in the refrigerator to make meringues for Baked Alaska or macaroons.

ALMOND CRUST ICE CREAM PIE

Serves 8-10

Substitute toasted pecans or macadamia nuts for almonds. Use any dense, good quality ice cream. Non-dairy works too. Try swirling two flavors together in the pie plate with a butter knife.

1-1/2 cups almonds, coarsely chopped
2-3 pints dense vanilla ice cream or
non-dairy "ice cream"

berries, peaches, apricots
mint leaves, for garnish

Toast chopped almonds on a cookie sheet for 10 minutes at 350 degrees. Remove and cool completely.

Soften ice cream in refrigerator until spreadable.

Distribute 1 cup chopped almonds evenly in pie plate. Spoon softened ice cream over almonds. Compress and smooth using a rubber spatula.

Sprinkle remaining almonds over pie. Cover with plastic wrap and freeze two hours before serving. Ice cream pie may be prepared ahead and frozen for up to 1 week.

When ready to serve, soften pie in refrigerator 20 minutes. Serve in small wedges garnished with a few perfect berries, or slices of peach or apricot and add a few mint leaves.

BAKED ALASKA MINIATURES

Serves 8   *Bake at 350, 450*

Chewy oatmeal cookies topped with ice cream and sorbet, transported into Baked Alaska heaven! Easy to serve.

Cookies

1/2 cup honey or fruit concentrate	*1 cup w/w pastry flour*
1/2 cup sweet butter or canola oil	*1/2 teaspoon salt*
□	*1 teaspoon baking powder*
2 eggs	*1 teaspoon cinnamon*
1/4 cup milk or soy milk	*1 cup rolled oats*

Preheat oven to 350 degrees. Grease two cookie sheets.

Cream honey and butter on high speed with an electric mixer. Add remaining ingredients with mixer on low speed. Incoporate just until oats are moistened.

Drop enough batter to make 8 cookies onto cookie sheets, flattening slightly. Bake 20 minutes or until lightly browned. Take sheets from oven and place on wire racks for 5 minutes before removing cookies from sheets with metal spatula to finish cooling on racks.

For the Baked Alaskas

8 oatmeal cookies	*8 egg whites*
2 pints dense vanilla ice cream	*1/4 cup honey or fruit*
or non-dairy ice cream	*juice concentrate*
1 cup raspberry sorbet	

Place cookies on a baking sheet.

Soften vanilla ice cream and then top each cookie with a large scoopful. Flatten to conform to shape of cookie. Smear a thin layer of raspberry sorbet on ice cream and freeze cookies for 30 minutes.

Preheat oven to 450 degrees.

Using the electric mixer, beat egg whites until foamy. Gradually add honey, beating until stiff and shiny. Spoon meringue over cookies and ice cream, covering the edges of cookies completely. Run a spatula around to seal. Freeze 15 minutes, or up to several hours.

Place in center of hot oven and bake Alaskas 3-4 minutes - meringues will be golden. Serve immediately.

INDIAN PUDDING

Serves 12   *Bake at 350*

Indian pudding is one of the most traditional of Colonial desserts. We think our version one of the best!

1-1/2 cups cornmeal
8 cups lo-fat milk
☐
2 tablespoons butter
1/4 cup molasses
1/3 cup honey
1/2 cup maple syrup

1/4 teaspoon salt
1/2 teaspoon ginger
1-1/2 teaspoons cinnamon
☐
3 eggs, beaten
1 cup raisins

Preheat oven to 350 degrees.

Combine cornmeal and 3 cups milk in a saucepan and stir with a wire whisk until smooth. Add the remaining milk and cook over medium heat, whisking, until it thickens and mixture comes to a boil. Simmer 2 minutes. Remove from heat, stir in butter, sweetening and spices.

Whisk a little of the hot mixture into the eggs. Slowly add egg mixture back into hot cornmeal, stirring to prevent eggs from cooking. Stir in raisins.

Grease an 11x14 inch baking pan. Pour pudding into pan and bake one hour, or until set around edges and browned. Indian Pudding will continue to cook when removed from the oven, so it should not be completely set when you take it out.

Serve warm or at room temperature. Chill leftovers.

CAROB MOUSSE CAKE

Serves 12   *Bake at 325*

Mousse cake, custardy and soft. For a festive look, pipe whipped cream on top and garnish with toasted almond pieces.

1-1/4 cups ground almonds
☐
1 pound barley-malt sweetened carob block, broken into pieces, or carob chips or disks
1 cup whipping cream
☐
6 eggs

1 teaspoon vanilla
1/2 cup whole wheat pastry flour
1/4 cup honey
☐
whipped cream
toasted almonds

Preheat oven to 325 degrees. Grease a 9-inch springform pan. Press almonds onto bottom and 1-1/2 inches up sides.

Using the steel blade of a food processor, chop carob block. If using carob chips or disks, no chopping is necessary. In a small pot, bring whipping cream to a boil. With the food processor running, pour hot cream through the feedtube and blend until mixture is smooth.

Using an an electric mixer on low speed, beat eggs and vanilla for 2 minutes. Add flour and honey; beat on high for 10 minutes, or until batter is thick and lemon colored. Gradually add carob mixture into batter. Turn into prepared pan and bake 45 minutes, or until puffed on the outer third of top. Center will be slightly soft. Do not overbake; remember, cake should have the consistency of custard.

Do not remove cake from pan. Cool 3-4 hours or overnight. To serve, run knife around outside of cake and carefully remove sides of springform pan.

APRICOT SPICE CAKE WITH WALNUTS

Serves 12-14   *Bake at 350*

Moist and wonderful. Keeps well and serves many.

1-1/2 cups dried apricots
1-1/2 cups water
□
1 cup canola or safflower oil
1 cup rice syrup or barley malt
1 cup fruit concentrate or honey
1 tablespoon vanilla extract
3 eggs
1 cup sour milk or yogurt

2 cups w/w pastry flour
2 teaspoons cinnamon
2 teaspoons allspice
1 teaspoon nutmeg
1/2 teaspoon salt
1 teaspoon baking soda
□
2 cups walnuts, chopped

Simmer apricots in water until soft. Puree in blender or food processor, adding a tablespoon more water if necessary.

Preheat oven to 350 degrees.

Grease a 10-inch tube pan.

With an electric mixer, on low-medium speed, beat together oil, sweeteners, vanilla, eggs, sour milk or yogurt, and apricot puree.

Mix in dry ingredients using low speed. Then incorporate walnuts.

Pour batter into pan and bake 45 minutes, or until a knife inserted in the center of the cake comes out clean. Remove cake from oven and let cool for 15 minutes in the pan on a rack. Remove cake from the pan to finish cooling on rack.

PRUNE GINGER CAKE

Serves 12   *Bake at 350*

Richly dark and very flavorful. A favorite.

1 cup dried prunes	**2 tablespoons carob powder**
□	**1 teaspoon cinnamon**
1/2 cup canola oil	**1/2 teaspoon cloves**
1 cup honey or fruit concentrate	**1/2 teaspoon ginger**
□	**1/2 teaspoon allspice**
1 egg	**1/2 teaspoon salt**
1/2 cup molasses or rice syrup	□
□	**1-1/2 teaspoons baking soda**
2-1/2 cups w/w pastry flour	**1 cup hot water**

Simmer prunes in 1-1/2 cups water until soft, about 15 minutes. Puree in a blender with cooking water. Set aside.

Preheat oven to 350 degrees. Grease a tube pan. Set aside.

Using an electric mixer, cream oil and honey until light. Beat in egg, molasses, and prune puree.

Fold dry ingredients, except baking soda, into wet. Dissolve baking soda in hot water and add to batter. Beat for several minutes.

Pour batter into pan and bake 45 minutes, or until knife inserted in the center of the cake comes out clean. Remove cake from oven and cool 15 minutes in pan on a rack. Then turn cake out to finish cooling on rack.

BANANA PECAN CAKE

Serves 12   *Bake at 375*

An old-fashioned banana cake with a subtly-spiced maple pecan batter.

1-1/2 cups w/w pastry flour   *2 eggs*
1 cup ground pecans   *1/2 cup maple syrup*
2 teaspoons cinnamon   *1/2 cup canola oil*
1/2 teaspoon baking soda   □
1/2 teaspoon salt   *2 teaspoons vanilla*
                                   2 large mashed bananas

Preheat oven to 375 degrees.   Grease a sponge cake tin.

Mix the dry ingredients together and set aside.

Using an electric mixer, beat eggs, maple syrup and oil until thick and creamy. Add vanilla and mashed banana.

Add dry ingredients to mixing bowl and beat briefly, just until moistened.

Spoon batter into prepared cake tin and bake 30-45 minutes, or until a knife inserted into the center of the cake comes out clean. Batter will begin to pull away from sides of pan. Turn off oven, open door slightly, and cool cake for 15 minutes in oven. Remove and place cake pan on cooling rack.

When cake is completely cool, remove from pan and frost with an all-fruit jam or carob frosting.

CARROT APPLESAUCE CAKE WITH APRICOT GLAZE

Serves 10   *Bake at 350*

Another old-fashioned favorite with an update - no cream cheese frosting but a beautiful golden apricot glaze.

2 cups w/w pastry flour
1 cup oats
1 1/2 teaspoons baking powder
1 1/2 teaspoons baking soda
1 tablespoon cinnamon
1 teaspoon nutmeg
1 teaspoon salt
□
1 cup raisins

1-1/4 cup honey or fruit
    concentrate
1 teaspoon vanilla
1-2/3 cups applesauce
1 pound grated carrots
4 eggs
3/4 cup canola or safflower oil
□
1 cup all-fruit apricot jam

Preheat oven to 350 degrees.   Grease two 9-inch cake pans.

Mix the dry ingredients together. Mix wet and add to dry. Stir just until moistened.

Spoon batter into prepared pans and bake 60 minutes, or until knife inserted in the center comes out clean and cake pulls away from the sides of the pan.

Remove cakes from oven and place pans on cooling racks for 20 minutes. Remove cakes from pans to finish cooling on rack.

Place one cake layer, flat side up, on cake plate. Smear a thin layer of apricot jam over cake. Place second layer, rounded side up, on top of first layer. Spread with remainder of apricot jam, sealing top and sides. Decorate with pieces of apricot from jam.

GERMAN CAROB CAKE

A 3-layer cake to serve 12   *Bake at 350*

For those who miss decadent richness! For special occasions.

Cake
- 1 cup carob powder
- 1 cup boiling water
- □
- 2-3/4 cups w/w pastry flour
- 2 teaspoons baking soda
- 1/2 teaspoon salt
- 1/2 teaspoon baking powder

- □
- 1 cup butter
- 2 cups honey or fruit juice concentrate
- 4 eggs
- 2 teaspoons vanilla extract

Frosting
- 2/3 cup butter
- 1/2 cup maple syrup
- 1/2 cup honey or fruit concentrate
- 2 eggs
- 1-1/3 cups heavy cream

- 1 teaspoon vanilla extract
- □
- 2-2/3 cups unsweetened shredded coconut
- 1-1/3 cups chopped walnuts

Preheat oven to 350 degrees. Grease three 9-inch round cake pans.

Whisk carob powder with boiling water until smooth. Cool completely. Mix dry ingredients in a bowl and set aside.

Using an electric mixer, cream butter, honey, eggs, and vanilla until thick and creamy. Add dry ingredients alternately with carob mixture to creamed batter. Mix only enough to moisten dry ingredients.

Divide batter between cake pans. Bake for 25-30 minutes, or until cake springs back when gently pressed with finger. Remove pans from oven and place on racks. Allow to stand 20 minutes before removing cakes to cool completely on racks.

While cake cools, prepare frosting.

Combine all ingredients except coconut and walnuts in a heavy-bottomed saucepan. Cook over medium heat, stirring, until mixture comes to a boil and begins to thicken. Remove saucepan from heat and stir in coconut and walnuts. Cool to room temperature before using on cake.

When cake and frosting are cool, frost between layers, on top, and lightly on sides.

Serve small slices as this cake is very rich.

BRANDY WALNUT FRUITCAKE

Makes 2 cakes, 12 servings each   *Bake at 275*

No artificially colored fruits, and the flavors are outstanding. Fruitcakes improve with age and will keep for a year.

1-1/2 cups date pieces in oat flour	**1 teaspoon cinnamon**
2/3 cup whole wheat pastry flour	**2 teaspoons allspice**
	1/2 teaspoon salt
	☐
1 cup dried pineapple pieces	**1 cup sweet butter (2 sticks)**
1 cup dried papaya	**1/2 cup honey**
1 cup raisins	**1/4 cup molasses**
☐	**6 eggs, separated**
2 cups walnut pieces	**1 tablespoon vanilla**
☐	☐
1-2/3 cups w/w pastry flour	**1/2 cup brandy**

Grease two 9x5x3 loaf tins.

Place dates in large mixing bowl or pot. Using the steel blade of a food processor, coarsely chop dried pineapple pieces with 1/3 cup flour and on/off turns. Add to dates. Chop papaya with 1/3 cup flour and add to bowl together with raisins.

Coarsely chop walnuts with steel blade and several on/off turns. Add to the dried fruit and mix thoroughly.

Combine remaining 1-2/3 cups flour with the spices and salt. Set aside.

Preheat oven to 275 degrees.

Using an electric mixer, cream butter on medium speed. Gradually beat in honey and molasses, egg yolks and vanilla. Add flour-spice mixture and brandy alternately to butter batter, beating after each addition. Blend in dried fruit and chopped walnuts.

In a separate bowl, with a clean dry beater, beat egg whites on high until stiff, but not dry. Carefully fold whites into the batter with a wire whisk and turn into prepared pans.

Bake for 3 hours. Take pans out of oven and place on racks to cool cakes for 1 hour, then remove cakes from pan to finish cooling on rack.

Wrap cakes in several thicknesses of cheesecloth or linen kitchen towels which have been drenched in brandy. Then wrap in aluminum foil or place in large plastic containers or ziplock plastic bags, and store in a cool, dry place for a month or two. (A garage in winter is fine.)

Check fruit cakes every two weeks to make sure that towels are still moist. Moisten with brandy as necessary.

Fruitcake may be eaten after two weeks.

Substitute apple juice or cider for brandy for a non-alchoholic fruitcake.

HONEY WHOLE WHEAT SPONGECAKE

Serves 6   *Bake at 300*

Delicious served with fresh berries, even for breakfast!

6 eggs, separated   **2 teaspoons vanilla**
1 cup honey   **1-1/2 cups w/w pastry flour**
1/2 teaspoon salt

Preheat oven to 300 degrees.

Using an electric mixer, beat egg whites at the highest speed until soft peaks form. While still beating, drizzle in 1/2 cup honey and salt. Continue to beat until stiff peaks form, or until mixture clings to bowl.

In a second bowl, beat yolks with the same beaters, gradually adding the remaining honey and vanilla, until thick and light in color.

Using a wire whisk or a rubber spatula, fold yolk mixture into whites, gently, but quickly. Fold in flour. Turn batter into an ungreased nine-inch tube cake pan and bake one hour.

Remove cake pan from oven and invert to cool cake. When completely cool, loosen cake with a butter knife by running knife around the sides of the pan and the tube. Turn pan over onto hand and gently remove cake to a cake plate.

CAROB CAKE

Serves 8   *Bake at 325*

Rich, dark, wonderful. May be served with whipped cream.

1/2 cup carob powder   □
3/4 cup boiling water   **1 cup honey**
          □   **1/2 cup safflower oil**
1-1/2 cups w/w pastry flour   **8 eggs, separated**
1-1/2 teaspoons baking powder   □
1 teaspoon cinnamon   **3 teaspoons vanilla**
1 teaspoon salt

Preheat oven to 325 degrees. Whisk together carob powder and boiling water in small bowl until no lumps remain.

In a small bowl, combine flour, baking powder, cinnamon and salt.

Using an electric mixer, cream honey with oil on medium speed. Add yolks, one at a time. Blend in cooled carob mixture and vanilla. Add dry ingredients and beat until batter is smooth.

Beat whites in a clean bowl with clean beater on high speed. Remove bowl from mixer, pour carob batter over whites, and fold in quickly and gently using a wire whisk. Do not over blend.

Turn cake into ungreased 10-inch tube pan. Bake 1 hour. Remove pan from oven to stand 5-10 minutes on a wire rack and then invert to cool.   When cool, remove cake from pan by running a knife around the edges to loosen.

PECAN CRUST CHEESECAKE WITH FRESH PEACHES

Serves 12   *Bake at 300*

Crust
  1/2 cup toasted wheat germ
  1/2 cup pecans
  1/2 teaspoon cinnamon

Topping
  2 cups fresh peaches,
    peeled and sliced
  1/4 cup all-fruit
    strawberry jam

Filling
  2 pounds cottage cheese
  8 ounces cream cheese
  3/4 cup honey
  2 teaspoons vanilla
  1/4 cup w/w pastry flour
  6 large eggs

Preheat oven to 300 degrees.

Toast pecans on a cookie sheet for 15 minutes. Remove from oven and cool completely.

Butter a 9-inch springform pan.

Using the steel blade of a food processor, grind pecans, wheat germ and cinnamon. Turn into pan and gently shake to distribute.

Place filling ingredients in workbowl. Blend filling until smooth and no pieces of cream cheese remain. Stop the machine once or twice to scrape down sides of workbowl with a rubber spatula. Gently pour cheese batter over crust. (Some crust will rise at first.) Place cake in oven and bake 1 hour. Turn off heat, but leave oven door closed another 1-1/2 hours. Then, remove cake and cool completely before covering and storing overnight in the refrigerator.

To serve, run a knife around the sides of the pan and carefully open springform to remove cake to a serving plate.

In a small pot, melt jam and add sliced peaches. Toss gently. Place peaches in a decorative pattern on top of the cheesecake and serve.

Instead of peaches, try strawberries, kiwi, blueberries, or fresh apricots. Combine fruits to make a colorful design.

Cheesecake without fruit can be refrigerated 2-3 days. With a fruit topping, cheesecake should be served immediately.

POPPY SEED CHEESECAKE

Serves 12   *Bake at 350*

For poppy seed lovers, a beautiful cheesecake!

Filling
- 1 pound cream cheese, cut
  into pieces
- 1 pound cottage cheese
- 4 eggs
- 1/2 cup honey
- 1 tablespoon orange juice
- 1 teaspoon vanilla extract

Topping I
- 1 cup dark raisins
- 1/2 cup water
- 1-1/2 cups poppy seeds
- 1/2 cup milk
- 1/2 cup honey
- 1 teaspoon vanilla extract

Topping II
- 1/2 cup walnuts
- 1/2 cup w/w pastry flour
- 1 teaspoon cinnamon
- 2 tablespoons butter
- 1/4 cup honey

Preheat oven to 350 degrees.

Filling

Using the steel blade of a food processor, blend the filling until no lumps of cream cheese remain. Stop machine once or twice to scrape down the sides of the workbowl with a rubber spatula.

Pour cheese mixture into the springform pan and bake one hour. Remove cheesecake from oven. Allow to cool in pan on a rack while toppings are prepared.

Topping I

Chop raisins using the steel blade and place in a saucepan with water. Cook over medium heat until water has evaporated.

Crush poppy seeds in an electric coffee grinder or blender until they resemble a dark gray powder. Add poppyseeds, milk, and honey to raisins. Simmer 15 minutes, stirring, to prevent from sticking or burning. Topping will become quite thick.

Remove and cool. Stir in vanilla.

Spread poppy seed topping over cheesecake. Do not remove cake from the springform pan.

Topping II

Using the steel blade, coarsely chop walnuts together with flour and cinnamon by turning machine on and off 3 times. Push butter into walnuts and drizzle honey on top. Turn the machine on/off several times, until no pieces of butter remain and the mixture is a streusel topping. Crumble over poppy seed mixture.

Slide cake under the broiler and broil just until top browns - 1 or 2 minutes. Watch cake CAREFULLY because it browns QUICKLY!

Refrigerate cheesecake overnight in the springform pan. To serve, run knife around edges, carefully open springform and remove cake to a serving plate.

STRAWBERRY APRICOT TARTLETS

Makes 12 tartletts   *Bake at 400*

Individual tartlets are pretty and elegant to serve. Dried apricots and fresh strawberries make a mouth-watering combination.

Crust
2-1/2 cups w/w pastry flour
1/2 cup ground almonds
1/4 teaspoon cinnamon

1/4 teaspoon salt
1/2 cup canola oil
1/3 cup honey or fruit
concentrate

Preheat oven to 400 degrees.

In a bowl, blend together crust ingredients, which should hold together when a clump is pressed between fingers. If crust seems too dry, add a spoonful of water; if too wet, add a spoonful of flour. Grease 12 tartlet shells with removable bottoms. Divide and press dough into shells. Prick with a fork. Bake 15 minutes.

Remove tartlets from oven and cool completely before pressing bottom of forms up gently to unmold shells.

Filling
1-1/2 cups dried apricots,
snipped coarsely
1/2 cup apricot juice, or
mango or strawberry

4 teaspoons arrowroot
☐
1 pint strawberries
2 tablespoons all-fruit jam

Place apricots in juice with arrowroot. Bring to a boil over low heat. Stir and turn off heat. Allow apricot mixture to cool.

Divide apricot mixture between shells, place fresh berries on top and brush with melted jam.

FRUIT COMPOTE WITH BERRIES

Serves 12

Inspired by Grandma Ida. A variation on an old favorite, stewed fruit compote. The colors are rich and beautiful.

1 cup pitted prunes
1 cup dried apricots
1 cup dried peaches
1/4 cup dried pineapple
6 cups water

1 cinnamon stick
☐
1 cup fresh blueberries
1 cup fresh strawberries
1 ripe banana

In a large, heavy pot, combine prunes, apricots, peaches, and pineapple with water and cinnamon stick. Bring to a simmer. Turn off heat and cool compote.

Refrigerate overnight to let flavors ripen.

Thirty minutes before serving, spoon 1 cup compote per person in large bowl. Add berries. Slice in banana. Stir gently so as not to crush berries. Chill for 30 minutes and serve in dessert bowls.

Compote can be served without fresh fruit, useful in winter.

STRAWBERRIES WITH RASPBERRY SAUCE

Serves 4-6

Wonderful with a hint of almond flavoring!

10 ounces fresh/frozen raspberries
2 tablespoons honey or fruit
   concentrate
1 tablespoon lemon juice
   ☐
1 quart fresh strawberries
2 tablespoons honey or fruit juice
   concentrate

1/2 teaspoon almond extract
   ☐
slivered almonds, optional
vanilla ice cream, optional
whipped cream, optional

For sauce: Using the steel blade of a food processor or a blender, puree raspberries. Strain to remove seeds. Place in pot with sweetener and lemon juice. Bring to a slow boil and cook over low heat 2 minutes. Cool sauce and set aside.

Wash and hull strawberries. Gently toss strawberries with sweetener and almond extract. Pour cooled raspberry sauce over berries and chill, covered, for several hours before serving. Garnish with toasted, slivered almonds, or a dollop of ice cream or whipped cream.

Sliced fresh peaches or apricots may be substituted for strawberries.

APPLE BROWN BETTY

Serves 6   *Bake at 325*

Apple brown betty makes a great breakfast, too, with a mug of steaming herbal tea, a glass of milk or soy milk. May be served with whipped cream, or a la mode.

8-10 apples, peeled and sliced
1/2 cup all-fruit strawberry or
raspberry jam or jelly
□
1 cup nuts or seeds

1 cup oats or other grain flakes
such as spelt, triticale
2 tablespoons fruit concentrate
2 teaspoons cinnamon

Preheat oven to 325 degrees.

Combine apples with jam. Place in a 12 x 8-inch baking pan, pyrex dish, or deep pie plate.

Using the steel blade of a food processor, whirl nuts, oats, fruit concentrate, and cinnamon with quick on/off turns until mixture resembles coarse meal.

Crumble topping evenly over apples and place pan in the oven. Bake 30-45 minutes, or until topping is nicely browned and apples are soft and bubbly.

Serve warm or cold.

Our favorite apples to use with this are the tart ones. MacIntosh or Granny Smiths work well too.

PLUM AND BLUEBERRY CRISP

Serves 6-8   *Bake at 325, 350*

If you prefer your crisp warm, not to worry. Make ahead, if desired, and set aside. When ready for dessert, reheat at 350 degrees for 10 minutes.

Topping
   1/3 cup pecans, chopped
   □
   1 cup w/w pastry flour
   1/2 cup rolled oats
   1/2 cup honey or fruit
      concentrate

Fruit Filling
   3 cups prune plums,
      pitted and sliced
   3 cups blueberries
   1/4 cup honey or fruit
      concentrate
   1 tablespoon arrowroot
   1 teaspoon nutmeg

Preheat oven to 325 degrees. Spread pecans on a cookie sheet and toast in oven until lightly browned, about 5-8 minutes.

Increase oven temperature to 350 degrees.

In a bowl, toss plums with blueberries, sweetener, arrowroot and nutmeg. Spoon into a 2-1/2 quart deep baking dish.

In another bowl, blend chopped toasted pecans, flour, oats, and honey or fruit concentrate until the mixture resembles a streusel topping.

Crumble the topping evenly over fruit. Place baking dish on a cookie sheet in the oven and bake 45 minutes, or until fruit juice begins to bubble and top is lightly browned. (The cookie sheet will catch any drips and make cleanup easier.) Remove crisp from oven and cool on a rack. Serve warm.

APRICOT FLUFF

Serves 6

Mild and delicious. Great for those watching fat intake.

1 cup dried apricots	**2 tablespoons lemon juice**
2 cups water	**1 teaspoon almond extract**
□	□
1/2 cup honey	**4 egg whites**

In a saucepan, cover apricots with water, bring to a boil, and simmer gently 15 minutes or until apricots are soft.

Using a food processor or blender, blend apricots with 4 tablespoons of their cooking liquid, honey, lemon juice and almond extract. Cool in a large bowl.

With an electric mixer or hand beater, beat egg whites until stiff and fold gently into mixture with a rubber spatula. Spoon into a serving bowl or individual dessert glasses. Chill for 3 hours before serving as a light dessert.

RHUBARB WITH BARLEY

Serves 8-10

Also makes a refreshing breakfast!

1 quart rhubarb cut into
   1/2 inch pieces
3/4 cup raisins
3/4 cup dates rolled in oat flour
2 whole oranges, blended
2 quarts boiling water

☐
1 teaspoon salt
1/4 teaspoon red pepper
☐
2 cups cooked barley

Combine rhubarb, raisins, dates and blended orange in a saucepan. Pour boiling water over all. Add salt and cayenne.

Bring to a boil and simmer five minutes. Stir in cooked barley. Spoon rhubarb mixture into a bowl. Cool several hours or overnight in the refrigerator to give the flavors a chance to blend.

APPLE-CRANBERRY STREUSEL PIE

Serves 10   *Bake at 350*

Although best served warm, Apple-Cranberry Streusel Pie is also delicious served cold.

1 cup cranberries   **7 cups peeled, sliced apples**
1-1/2 cups all-fruit   **1 teaspoon cinnamon**
  strawberry jam

Topping
  1 cup desiccated coconut
  1/4 cup oats   **3/4 cup sesame seeds**
  2 tablespoons honey   **or almond meal**

Preheat oven to 350 degrees.

Combine cranberries, jam, apples and cinnamon. Place pie filling in a tart pan, pie plate or 10-inch oven-proof skillet.

Using the steel blade of a food processor, blend topping and crumble evenly over pie.

Place pie plate on a cookie sheet to bake 45 minutes in the oven, or until fruit is bubbly and top lightly browned. (A cookie sheet will catch drips and make cleanup easier.)

OLD-FASHIONED PECAN PIE

Serves 6   *Bake at 350*

New England farm cooks of old used maple syrup in large amounts. Here, maple syrup is "cut" with the addition of barley malt and carob, which gives the pie a luscious, thick richness without butter.

1 unbaked 9-inch w/w pie crust
□
1 cup maple syrup
1/2 cup barley malt syrup
4 eggs, beaten

1 tablespoon whole wheat flour
1 tablespoon carob powder
1/4 teaspoon salt
1/2 teaspoon nutmeg
□
1 cup pecans

Using an electric mixer, food processor, or a wooden spoon, beat all ingredients, except the pecans, together. Stir in pecans and pour pie filling into crust.

Place pie plate on cookie sheet to bake in oven for 1 hour at 350 degrees, or until pie is slightly firm to touch and nicely browned. The cookie sheet will catch the drips and make cleanup easier.

The pecans will rise to top of pie as it bakes. When the pie is baked, remove from the oven and cool on a rack.

SWEET POTATO PIE

Serves 6   *Bake at 450, 350*

Dedicated to Andrea Morgan, one of our original crew who was delighted not to have to peel pumpkin. Unusually wholesome and delicious - great even for breakfast! A pound of tofu can be substituted for the eggs and milk.

1 unbaked 9-inch w/w pie crust	**2 teaspoons vanilla extract**
□	**1 teaspoon cinnamon**
3 pounds (about 3-1/2 cups)	**1/2 teaspoon ground cloves**
** sweet potatoes, boiled soft**	**1/2 teaspoon allspice**
1 cup milk or soy milk	**1/4 teaspoon nutmeg**
3 eggs, beaten	**1/4 teaspoon ginger**
1/2 cup maple syrup	**1/4 teaspoon salt**

Preheat oven to 450 degrees.

Using the steel blade of a food processor, blend sweet potatoes (don't peel) together with remaining ingredients until the batter is smooth and flows easily under the blade.

Pour mixture into unbaked crust. Place pie in oven and bake at 450 degrees for 10 minutes, then reduce oven temperature to 350 degrees and bake an additional 45 minutes, or until pie is set.

Take pie out of oven and set on a rack. Cool before cutting. Serve plain or with a whipped topping.

BLUEBERRY PIE

Serves 6   *Bake at 350*

Our adaptation of a favorite from the Deaf Smith Country Cookbook. Adding thyme makes cultivated blueberries taste like wild ones.

1 unbaked 9-inch whole wheat pie crust	1 tablespoon lemon juice
6 cups fresh or frozen blueberries	1/2 teaspoon nutmeg
4 tablespoons whole wheat flour	2 tablespoons arrowroot
1/2 cup pure maple syrup	pinch sea salt
	pinch thyme

Preheat oven to 350 degrees.

Mix berries with the remaining ingredients and spoon into crust. Let stand 15 minutes.

Place pie on a cookie sheet to make carrying to the oven easier and to catch blueberry drips while pie bakes!

Bake 1-1/2 hours, or until crust begins to brown and blueberries begin to firm. (Pie will solidify somewhat as it cools.)

Remove cookie sheet from oven and cool pie on a wire rack. Serve blueberry pie warm, room temperature, or cold.

Substitute pitted cherries or sliced peaches for blueberries.

Miscellaneous

MISCELLANEOUS

Our catch-all. Where else could we fit in dill pickles, homemade yogurt, fruit smoothies and apple cider syrup?

PUMPKIN SEED PESTO

Makes about 3 cups

Zippy and tart, a different kind of pesto.

**2 cups packed parsley
  leaves
1 tablespoon dried cilantro
3/4 cup pumpkin seeds,
  roasted on cookie sheet
  350 degrees for 5 minutes
1/2 cup grated Pecorino
  Romano cheese**

**1/2 cup fresh lime juice
1 jalapeno pepper, seeded
3 cloves garlic
  □
3/4 cup olive oil
salt and black pepper to taste**

Using the steel blade of a food processor, blend parsley, cilantro, pumpkin seeds, Romano, lime juice, jalapeno and garlic, stopping the machine once or twice to scrape down the sides of workbowl with a rubber spatula. With the machine running, gradually add oil and blend until smooth. Season to taste with salt and pepper.

Pumpkin seed pesto can be prepared 3-4 days ahead. Press plastic wrap onto surface of pesto to store. Cover tightly and refrigerate. Bring to room temperature before serving.

Serve over beans or rice. Also good on chicken and fish.

SUMMER PESTO

Makes about 3 cups

Serve pesto with fettuccine, use in calzones, or stir a spoonful into stews or soups. Use to season fish or poultry.

Store pesto in small glass jars in the refrigerator for several days, or make pesto "ice cubes" and store in plastic baggies in the freezer.

2 cups packed parsley *1/2 teaspoon black pepper*
1 large bunch fresh basil *1/4 teaspoon cayenne pepper*
1/2 cup olive oil *1/2 teaspoon oregano*
4 cloves garlic *1/2 cup pine nuts or walnuts*
1/2 cup grated Pecorino Romano

Using the steel blade of a food processor, blend ingredients until smooth, stopping the machine as needed to scrape down the sides of the workbowl with a rubber spatula.

Pesto is wonderful. Always have some on hand to dress up a plain dish. Make in the summer when fresh basil is plentiful.

WINTER PESTO

Makes about 4-1/2 cups

Winter pesto reminds one of summer. So let it snow and have the best of both seasons!

12 ounces fresh spinach
1 bunch parsley
1/3 cup lemon juice
1 cup olive oil
2/3 cup pine nuts or
**   almonds or walnuts**

1 cup grated Pecorino Romano
1/3 cup dried basil
6 cloves garlic
1/4 teaspooon cayenne
1 teaspoon black pepper

Wash the spinach and parsley and spin-dry in a salad spinner.

Using the steel blade of a food processor, blend half the spinach and parsley with the remaining ingredients. When the mixture is smooth, add remaining greens. Process until pesto is a paste.

Use winter pesto just as you would summer pesto.

DEBRA'S OLIVE OIL VINAIGRETTE

Makes 6 cups

Worth making a large batch to keep in the refrigerator so that dressing will always be ready when you are!

4 cups olive oil
1 cup lemon juice
1 cup cider vinegar
10 cloves garlic, mashed
   in garlic press

2 teaspoons salt
2 teaspoons black pepper
1/2 teaspoon each basil,
   oregano, thyme
1 teaspoon mustard powder

Combine all dressing ingredients with a wire whisk in a bowl. Or, whisk everything together in an 8-cup measuring cup, which saves having to wash extra measuring cups.

Keep dressing ready in jars in the refrigerator, where it may cloud up or become semi-solid because of the cold. Bring to room temperature and shake before using.

MUSTARD MARINADE

Makes about 1 cup marinade

1 onion, quartered
1 teaspoon dried parsley
2 tablespoons Dijon mustard

4 tablespoons lemon juice
1 tablespoon thyme
1 teaspoon tarragon

Using the steel blade of a food processor, or a blender, blend ingredients. Use to pour over chicken, fish or tofu and marinate for at least 30 minutes. Broil chicken, fish or tofu in marinade.

8 CALORIES PER TABLESPOON AND A HALF: 2 G CARBOHYDRATE; 36 MG SODIUM; 0 MG CHOLESTEROL

GINGER MARINADE

Makes about 1 cup marinade

1 onion, quartered
2 cloves garlic
1 teaspoon ginger

2 tablespoons tamari soy sauce
1 teaspoon lemon juice

Using the steel blade of a food processor, or a blender, blend marinade. Use to pour over chicken, fish or tofu and marinate for at least 30 minutes. Broil chicken, fish or tofu in marinade.

7 CALORIES PER TABLESPOON AND A HALF: 2 G CARBOHYDRATE; 172 MG SODIUM; 0 MG CHOLESTEROL

HERB-INFUSED OIL

Fill a bottle half full of washed and dried fresh herb leaves. Fill bottle with olive oil. Cover tightly and steep for a week or two in a cool, dark place. Strain oil into another jar or bottle. Add several sprigs of herbs before covering and storing in the refrigerator.

Try combinations of herbs and some lemon wedges too.

FRUIT FLAVORED VINEGAR

In an enamel or stainless steel pan, bring 1 quart cider vinegar to a simmer. Add 2 cups berries and let mixture stand off the heat for 10 minutes. Pour vinegar and fruit into a jar and cover. Steep for 10-20 days and enjoy liberally. This is especially beautiful with raspberries. Try this with rose petals from unsprayed roses as well.

HERB FLAVORED VINEGAR

Spread washed and dried fresh herb leaves on a cookie sheet. Dry away from sunlight until the leaves begin to curl. In a jar, place one cup packed herbs leaves together with one pint cider vinegar. Cover. Let jar stand for two weeks on a sunny window ledge. Shake jar once or twice each day. When the flavor is strong enough for your taste, strain into a clean jar, add herbs if desired and begin to use.

HORSERADISH

Makes a lot! (Depends upon the root you choose.)

Be careful when making horseradish! Follow the directions below. If you like the red variety, add half a fresh beet. Horseradish prepared this way will keep for months in the refrigerator.

1 large horseradish root	**2 teaspoons salt**
1-1/4 cups cider vinegar	

Scrub horseradish root with a stiff-bristled brush to remove dirt. Peel it and cut into 1-inch pieces.

Using the steel blade of a food processor and on/off turns, chop horseradish. With the machine running, add vinegar and salt. Process until horseradish is smooth.

Do not open workbowl for 5 minutes to give the fumes a chance to settle. If the root is a powerful one and the lid is removed too soon, your eyes will tear and your throat will burn. Be careful!

Spoon horseradish into glass jars and store in the refrigerator. Horseradish may "burn" the inside of metal jar covers and the top of the horseradish may brown over time as it dries out, but the underneath layers will still be fine and potent enough to use.

Use horseradish in Debra's Famous Cold Remedy, as well as to accompany fish or chicken.

SOY NUTS

Makes about 6 cups   *Toast at 350*

3 cups dried soybeans   **1 tablespoon tamari**
5 cups water   **soy sauce, optional**

Soak soybeans overnight in enough water to cover by 3 inches. Check and add more water if necessary.

After soaking, bring soybeans and water to a boil and simmer 15 minutes with the pot covered, just to soften. Skim off foam and hulls that float to the surface. Drain soybeans and mix with tamari if a somewhat salty taste is desired.

Spread beans on cookie sheets and toast in the oven until golden brown, stirring frequently, about 45-60 minutes. Remove from oven to cool completely before storing in jars.

194 CALORIES PER 1/2 CUP: 17 G PROTEIN; 14 G CARBOHYDRATE; 9 G FAT; 1 MG SODIUM; 0 MG CHOLESTEROL

ROASTED CHICKPEAS

Makes about 2-2/3 cups   *Bake at 350*

1-1/2 cups chickpeas   **garlic powder, optional**
2 tablespoons tamari   **cayenne pepper, optional**
soy sauce, optional

Wash and sort beans. Cook according to your favorite method until chickpeas are tender. Mix with seasonings to taste. Spread beans out on cookie sheets and roast in a 350 oven, stirring frequently, for 45-60 minutes, or until browned and crisp.

Remove beans from oven to cool completely before storing in a jar.

FIERY HOT CHILE SAUCE

Makes about 2/3 cup

This recipe doubles easily. Use over rice, beans, millet, grilled poultry or fish.

8-10 dried hot red chiles,
  preferably guajillo or chipotle
2 tablespoons olive oil
6 cloves garlic

1 teaspoon ground coriander
1 teaspoon ground caraway
1/2 teaspoon salt
2 tablespoons water

Stem and seed chiles. Break into pieces. Rinse under cold water. Let chiles stand 5 minutes. Do not pat dry.

Using the steel blade of a food processor, blend chiles, oil, garlic, coriander, caraway and salt to paste. Some texture should remain. Add water with quick on-off turns.

Fiery Hot Chile Sauce can be prepared a week ahead and covered and refrigerated. Thin with water if necessary before using.

GARLIC SAUCE

Makes about 3/4 cup

A nice simple sauce to use as a last-minute marinade.

4 cloves garlic
1/2 cup olive oil

1/4 cup lemon juice
salt and red pepper to taste

Using a food processor or blender, blend ingredients until smooth.

Use garlic sauce to brush chicken or fish before broiling or while grilling, or serve garlic sauce as a main course dip at the table.

Store in a glass jar in the refrigerator. Nice to have on hand to spice up an otherwise plain dish!

Try adding orange juice in place of lemon, 1/4 cup tomato juice, a teaspoon each paprika, cumin, oregano, pepper and the 4 cloves garlic to make a Mexican Sauce for Marinade.

OLD-FASHIONED DILL PICKLES

Makes lots of pickles

Cut cucumbers into 2-inch chunks, or leave whole. Grape leaves are used as a natural preservative and to keep pickles firm.

1-1/2 quarts cider vinegar	**1 cup fresh dill weed**
4 quarts water	**12 cloves peeled garlic**
fresh grape leaves	**3 bay leaves**
6 pounds pickling cucumbers	**2 tablespoons black**
1-1/2 cups salt	**peppercorns**

Combine water and vinegar.

Place some grape leaves on the bottom of glass jars or a large ceramic crock. Pack container(s) with cucumbers. Fill with vinegar and water, adding more water if necessary for container to be full. Pour liquid off cucumbers (Now you have the exact amount.) into the pan. Bring liquid to a boil. Add salt and stir until dissolved.

Add dill, garlic, bay leaves, and peppercorns to cucumbers. Cover with more grape leaves. Pour brine over cucumbers so that pickles and leaves are completely covered. Use a heavy, clean stone or dish to keep cucumbers submerged if not wedged tightly under liquid.

Set jars or crock aside, covered, for 2 days. After 2 days, refrigerate pickles. They are ready to start eating when half-sour, after a day.

Reuse brine to pickle Jerusalem artichokes or other vegetables.

APPLE CIDER SYRUP

Makes about 4 cups

To make cider syrup, fresh cider, juiced not more than 1/2 hour prior to boiling must be used, otherwise the necessary pectin will not be active.

Use cider syrup as you would maple syrup.

Enough apples to juice to make one gallon cider

Using a vegetable juicer, juice enough apples to make 1 gallon cider.

Boil cider at about 219 degrees until reduced to syrup. (Cider is acidic and should be boiled in stainless steel or enamel pots only.)

Boiling to the syrup stage will take several hours. To reduce boiling time, partially freeze cider. Use the sweet portion, which freezes last, for boiling.

When the cider is reduced to syrup, store in glass jars in the refrigerator.

RAW CRANBERRY RELISH

Makes about 10 cups

A nice change from cooked and sugared cranberry sauce. Cranberry relish keeps for two weeks in the refrigerator and also freezes well.

4 cups raw cranberries
3 medium oranges, quartered,
   seeded and peeled
3 large apples, quartered, cored
   and peeled

1 cup honey or fruit juice
   concentrate
1/2 teaspoon cinnamon

Using the steel blade of a food processor, coarsely chop cranberries, oranges, and apples with on/off turns. Stop the machine once or twice to scrape down the sides of the workbowl with a rubber spatula.

Put the chopped fruit in a large bowl. Add honey and cinnamon and mix well. Refrigerate cranberry relish in glass jars.

In addition to serving cranberry relish with poultry, try mixing with unflavored yogurt for a quick snack.

JAN'S ZAATAR

Makes about 2-1/4 cups

This comes from Lebanon. Use over salad, rice, beans, fish, chicken. Zaatar is said to aid digestion and to clear up skin problems!

4 tablespoons brown sesame   1 cup ground sumac
   seeds   2 tablespoons salt
1 cup oregano

In a skillet, dry roast sesame seeds over low heat until they become fragrant and begin to pop. Add oregano, sumac and salt and stir 1 minute. Remove from heat.

Cool and store zaatar in glass jars. Use as you would salt.

GOMASIO

Makes 4-1/2 cups

Gomasio is a sesame flavored salt. Sesame seeds are an excellent source of protein and are rich in calcium.

1/2 cup sea salt   **4 cups whole brown sesame seeds**

Heat salt in a large skillet over a moderate flame. Set aside in a bowl.

Toast sesame seeds in the same skillet, stirring over medium-high heat for 5-10 minutes until slightly browned and aromatic. Seeds will begin to pop. Be careful not to burn!

Coarsely grind sesame seeds and salt using the steel blade of a food processor and on/off turns.

Store gomasio in airtight containers (Glass jars are good.). A teaspoon of brown rice may be added to absorb any moisture and prevent clumping.

Use gomasio as you would salt, on salad, over cooked vegetables, grains, fish, or poultry.

HERBED BUTTER

Makes 1 cup herb butter

**1 cup (2 sticks) unsalted sweet
  butter, room temperature
1/2 teaspoon oregano
1/2 teaspoon thyme**

**1 tablespoon snipped fresh
  chives
1 tablespoon watercress leaves**

Soften butter. Whip using the steel blade of a food processor and on/off turns until butter is smooth. Add remaining ingredients and mix in with on/off turns.

Transfer butter to a small bowl where it will keep several days in the refrigerator. Bring butter to room temperature before serving.

Feel free to substitute tarragon for oregano. Or add garlic or onion powder to butter to spread on breads.

Substitute your favorite herbs for the ones listed above.

HONEY BUTTER

Remember Sue Maid brand honey butter in the pretty, short, fat pastel jars? Make your own!

1/2 cup butter   **1/4 cup honey**

Cream the butter using the steel blade of a food processor until smooth and soft. Add honey and whip until fluffy.

Store in small covered crocks or glass jars in the refrigerator.

Use honey butter on toast, pancakes, or waffles.

For variety, add rind of half an orange while processing. Try 1/4 teaspoon cinnamon or nutmeg, or several toasted almonds.

CREAM WITH HONEY AND SPICES

1 cup heavy cream   **1/2 teaspoon cinnamon or**
3 tablespoons honey   **nutmeg**

Using an electric mixer, beat cream until lightly thickened. Beat in honey and cinnamon or nutmeg.

Serve as a topping with pumpkin pie, fruit pies, or gingerbread.

PEACH AND RASPBERRY JAM

Makes 1-1/2 cups

2 cups peaches, halved, peeled,
and pitted
1 cup fresh raspberries
1/3 cup honey or fruit concentrate

2 tablespoon brandy, optional
☐
1/4 teaspoon almond extract

Coarsely chop peaches using the steel blade of a food processor and several on/off turns.

In a small, heavy saucepan combine the peaches, raspberries, honey and brandy, if desired. Bring to a boil over moderate heat and stir until thickened, about 15 minutes.

Cool jam. Add almond extract, cover and refrigerate. Will keep for up to 10 days.

HONEY PLUM JAM

Makes 1-1/2 cups

**3 cups prune plums, halved
    and pitted**

**1/4 cup cider vinegar
1/4 cup honey**

Coarsely chop plums using the steel blade of a food processor and on/off turns.

In a small, heavy saucepan, combine plums, cider vinegar and honey. Bring to a boil over moderate heat. Reduce heat to low and simmer until thick, stirring, about 10-15 minutes.

Remove pot from heat. Cool jam, cover and refrigerate for up to 10 days.

ALMOND BUTTER

Makes 1 cup   *Roast at 300*

1-1/2 cups almonds   **1 tablespoon tahini, optional**

Preheat oven to 300 degrees.

Roast almonds on a cookie sheet in oven for 10-20 minutes. Watch carefully so they do not burn.

Place all but 1/4 cup of the almonds in the workbowl of a food processor fitted with the steel blade, or in a blender. Blend until smooth. Chop the reserved nuts into nut butter with several on/off turns of either machine.

Almonds can be also ground into nut butter without roasting first. If nut butter is not "liquidy" enough, add 1 tablespoon tahini.

Cashew butter: Roast cashews 10-15 minutes. Blend until the consistency desired. Chop in 1/4 cup of the nuts at the last minute for chunky-style nut butter.

Peanut butter: Roast peanuts for 20 minutes. Blend until the consistency desired. Also chop in 1/4 cup of the nuts at the last minute for chunky-style nut butter.

To make a sweet nut butter, blend in honey and a dash of cinnamon to taste.

MAKING YOUR OWN YOGURT

Makes 1 quart

1 quart low-fat or skim milk	**3 tablespoons yogurt, or**
1/2 cup non-instant milk	**1 package dried yogurt culture**
powder, optional	

Scald milk, but do not boil. Cool to lukewarm. If a thicker yogurt is desired, blend some milk with milk powder and add back to pot. Stir in yogurt or culture.

Pour mixture into clean glasses or jars. Cover jars tightly. Set in a large pan of water or in a yogurt maker. If you are NOT using a yogurt maker, place pan in a warm oven. Maintain the temperature of the water at about 100 degrees.

Leave the yogurt alone for at least 2 hours. Moving it or tipping the container to peek at it during the first incubation will break up the custard and make it watery.

The yogurt will take 3-5 hours to thicken. Dried culture takes about an hour longer. Remove jars from incubator or water. Refrigerate. Yogurt will settle and thicken more as it cools. It can also be left to sit overnight and refrigerated in the morning.

Save 1/4 cup of yogurt each time to make the next batch. Use new starter within 5 days. The fresher the yogurt the more effective it is as a starter.

MAYONNAISE

Makes 1 cup

1 egg	**1 tablespoon lemon juice**
1/2 teaspoon salt	**1 cup oil (olive, almond, walnut,**
1/2 teaspoon dry mustard	**or safflower), at room**
1 tablespoon cider vinegar	**temperature**

Using the steel blade of a food processor, blend egg, salt, mustard, vinegar, lemon juice and a few drops of oil.

With the machine running, slowly pour remaining oil through the feed tube in a steady stream. That's all there is to it!

Store mayonnaise in a glass jar in the refrigerator until ready to use.

For a thicker mayonnaise, add 1/4 cup more oil.

Other options: Leave out mustard; try adding a teaspoon of honey or more to taste. Use safflower oil when making a sweetened or milder mayonnaise.

To make "green" mayonnaise, chop 1-1/2 cups combined and loosely packed watercress, tarragon, chives, or parsley with the food processor. Strain mixture through a fine-meshed strainer or cheesecloth. Mix juice into mayonnaise. (Reserve greens for use in soup or stews.)

DEBRA'S FAMOUS COLD REMEDY

Enough medicine to kill many colds

This remedy works! My son, Adam, says I used to torture him with it when he was too little to appreciate its effectiveness. My brother, Daniel, took it on a bike trip to Nova Scotia and said it saved his vacation. If your throat hurts too much to swallow, this will act like balm.

1 cup raw honey
1-2 tablespoons cayenne pepper

1-2 tablespoons prepared horseradish

Place honey in a glass jar. Add pepper and horseradish. Stir until liquidy.

Store cold remedy in the refrigerator until you feel something coming on or have a sore throat. When you use this remedy, take a 1/16 teaspoon dose or just a tiny dot. True, you will feel the heat and may think you are dying, but the honey will coat the throat, the red pepper will warm it and stop the hurt. We all know that horseradish opens blocked passages. Cayenne pepper is rich in vitamin C, higher even than orange juice.

Take remedy as needed.

So, stop laughing and mix some up today when you're feeling healthy. When you're sick, you won't feel like doing anything.

FRUIT SMOOTHIE

Makes 2 drinks

2 bananas
2 cups milk or soy milk
1 teaspoon vanilla
2 eggs, placed in boiling
  water for 30 seconds and
  removed

2 tablespoons honey or
  maple syrup
1/2 teaspoon brewers yeast

Using an electric blender, blend all ingredients until no pieces of banana remain. Chill drink 1 hour. Blend again for several seconds and serve in tall frosty glasses.

Frozen bananas may be used to eliminate chilling time. Freeze bananas when ripe. (Peel and place in the freezer on cookie sheets. Once frozen, remove from cookie sheets and store in plastic bags.

FRUIT SMOOTHIE VARIATION

Makes 2 drinks

2 ripe bananas
2/3 cup papaya juice

4 cups mixed fruit, some
frozen

Using an electric blender, blend all ingredients until no pieces of banana remain. Serve in tall frosty glasses.

We like to freeze cut-up watermelon to make the smoothie very refreshing. Strawberries and blueberries give the drink a beautiful rosy color. Using mostly frozen fresh fruit results in a wonderful, thick smoothie, almost like ice cream. Use a rubber spatula to help the blender cope with all that frozen fruit.

STRAWBERRY ORANGE COOLER

Makes 2 drinks

1 pint frozen strawberries
1 cup orange juice
1 cup yogurt

2 tablespoons honey or
   more to taste
1/2 teaspoon brewers yeast

Using an electric blender, blend all ingredients until the berries move smoothly under the blade.

Serve at once in tall frosty glasses.

Strawberries can be purchased frozen, or frozen when they are plentiful in the summer. Wash, hull and place on cookie sheets in the freezer. Once frozen, remove and store in air-tight containers or plastic bags.

235 CALORIES PER SERVING: 8 G PROTEIN, 3 G FAT, 32 G CARBOHYDRATE; 87 MG SODIUM; 0 MG CHOLESTEROL

NUT MILKS

Makes about 5 cups

1 cup nuts, almond
   cashew, peanut, or
   sunflower

3-4 cups water
4 pitted dates

Using an electric blender, liquefy nuts and water until a milky consistency. Adding the dates makes the milk sweeter and thicker.

MEASURING SIMPLIFIED

1 teaspoon	= 1/3 tablespoon
1 tablespoon	= 3 teaspoons
2 tablespoons	= 1 fluid ounce
4 tablespoons	= 1/4 cup
5-1/3 tablespoons	= 1/3 cup or 2-2/3 ounces
8 tablespoons	= 1/2 cup
16 tablespoons	= 1 cup
1 cup	= 1/2 pint or 8 fluid ounces
2 cups	= 1 pint or 16 fluid ounces
1 pint liquid	= 16 fluid ounces or 2 cups
1 quart liquid	= 2 pints or 4 cups
1 gallon	= 4 quarts
16 dry ounces	= 1 pound
1 stick butter	= 8 tablespoons
4 cups flour	= 1 pound
8 ounce can	= 1 cup
one ounce	= 6 teaspoons, 2 tablespoons, 1/8 cup
2 cups liquid	= 1 pound

6 1/2-inch slices dry bread = 1 cup breadcrumbs
1/2 pint cream = 1 cup or 2 cups whipped
1 pound nutmeats = 4-1/2 cups, about 3-1/2 cups chopped

1/2 whole egg = about 2 tablespoons
5 whole eggs = 1 cup
8-9 whites = 1 cup
12 yolks = 1 cup

INDEX

BREADS, continued

SOUPS

SOUPS, continued

SALADS

SALADS, continued

BEAN AND GRAIN SALADS

PASTA AND CHEESE MAIN DISHES

PASTA AND CHEESE MAIN DISHES, continued

BEAN AND GRAIN MAIN DISHES

POULTRY MAIN DISHES

POULTRY MAIN DISHES, continued

SEAFOOD MAIN DISHES

DESSERTS

DESSERTS, continued

MISCELLANEOUS

MISCELLANEOUS, continued

NOTES

NOTES